Housebreak
Any Dog
The Permanent Three-Step Method

Audrey Carr with Lou Ellen Davis
Foreword by Anthony Miele, D.V.M.

CB
CONTEMPORARY BOOKS

Library of Congress Cataloging-in-Publication Data

Carr, Audrey, 1952–.
    Housebreak any dog : the permanent three-step method / Audrey Carr with
Lou Ellen Davis ; foreword by Anthony Miele.
      p.   cm.
    Includes index.
    ISBN 0-8092-3074-7
    1. Dogs—Training.   I. Davis, Lou Ellen, 1936–.   II. Title.
SF431.C375   1997
636.7′083—dc20   96-38852
                                                       CIP

Cover design by Kim Bartko
Cover photograph: Copyright © David B. Sutton
Interior design by Mary Lockwood

18   17   16   15   14   13   12   11   10   9   8   7   6   5   4   3   2   1

To the memory of my mother's love for dogs; and to "the sunlight in my universe," my son, Chris

Contents

Foreword

As founder and director of six busy New York City veterinary medical centers treating "any pet that fits through the door," for more than fifteen years I have cared for literally thousands of dogs and have answered thousands of dog-related questions. An extraordinary number of these questions have dealt with housebreaking.

Although problems in housebreaking dogs are common, rarely are they medically based. In virtually all cases, the difficulty lies with owners who are either poorly informed or who have not realized the critical need for consistency in using the right information once they do have it.

Nor has the "right" information always been easy to find. This is why, many years ago, I wrote a one-page synopsis of the techniques I recommend, which I still hand out today.

However, because housebreaking is not always simple, nor are any two dogs ever quite alike, for most owners one page is insufficient. For these reasons, in addition to the handout I commonly recommend both books and specific professional trainers. Although I have absolute confidence in the few trainers I regularly recommend, I must admit that none of the books I've recommended has fully satisfied me, until I read *Housebreak Any Dog*.

For close to fifteen years, Audrey Carr has been one of the top professionals I've recommended for dog training in all areas, but I virtually always recommend only her to those whose sole concern is housebreaking, because Audrey specializes in this area and is one of the few trainers I know who does not insist on selling a whole training "package." Instead, she always has been willing to tackle housebreaking exclusively. I have no doubt that her concentrated experience in this area has much to do with her exceptional expertise, as reflected by the original Three-Step Program, which she has developed over many years and now presents to the general public for the first time in print, in *Housebreak Any Dog*.

Housebreak Any Dog is firmly packed with solid information, much of it original and all of it clear, well organized, and uncompromising in its integrity. Audrey's "tough love" approach is gentle enough for the most timid toy, yet strong enough to work with a full-grown giant breed. In addition, the style of the book (hats off to coauthor Lou Ellen Davis, a longtime professional writer on many subjects) is delightful to read. It is well organized and clear, but also warm, supportive, and liberally sprinkled with short stories, which most readers will find easy to identify with or, at least, simply enjoy!

I strongly endorse *Housebreak Any Dog* and recommend it to every dog owner, whether the pet is a new pup or whether the issue is a "special problem," such as sudden regression in a much older animal. Audrey does an extraordinary job in covering all of it!

Anthony Miele, D.V.M.

Acknowledgments

My sincere appreciation to Harvey Rachlin, for his help and support and for introducing me to the magic of my coauthor.

Thank you to my sister, Eileen, for always being there.

Thanks go to my coauthor's son, Mike Davis, for sharing his computer know-how.

Thank you to my savvy editor, Alina Cowden, a true "dog person."

And finally, thanks to all my past and present four-legged cohabitants, from Todd to Sundance.

Introduction

The first time I saw Max—a medium-sized, floppy-eared, brown mutt with spots, large sad eyes, and no collar or ID—he was soaking wet, shivering in the rain outside a local supermarket. Because at that moment my primary concern was to avoid being reduced to the same condition, I loaded my groceries into the trunk and got behind the wheel as fast as possible. I felt bad about Max, but the world is full of stray dogs, and I already had twelve—count 'em, twelve!—dogs at home. My Doberman had just produced a litter of eight. I had my schnauzer and a stray female mutt I had picked up three weeks earlier. I also was boarding a springer spaniel that I was training for its owner. Further, my ten-year-old son, Chris, definitely deserved more of my time and attention than he'd been getting lately.

I pulled out into the late afternoon wet traffic.

The problem was that after ten minutes on the road, with a couple of pounds of frozen food in the trunk and the need to pick up Chris at a friend's house, put away the groceries, walk the adult dogs in the rain, cook dinner, do at least one load of laundry, and return half a dozen phone calls, I still couldn't get Max out of my mind.

Finally, despite the rain that was now so heavy I could hardly see, I pulled into the nearest driveway and turned around.

Max was still there, looking even wetter and sadder than before. Because strays often have had bad experiences with strangers, the first item on my agenda was figuring out how to get close to him without scaring him away. As a professional trainer, I knew I'd need to sound him out—to get a sense of his personality and then decide how to entice him into my arms. (In looking back, I suspect fate had set up the whole encounter.) I pulled in close to him, leaned over the seat, opened the passenger-side door, and made eye contact. That was all it took! He jumped in beside me, immediately shook water all over me, then tried to get onto my lap!

"No," I said. "Down." To my surprise, he turned into a perfect gentleman. Still dripping, he grinned at me but stayed entirely on his own side of the seat. Obviously, someone had invested a considerable amount of time and love in training him.

The next morning, I put up notices all over the shopping area describing this "lost" dog. No one claimed him, which eventually convinced me that he was not really lost but had been abandoned. I suspect that somewhere someone who'd cried him or herself to sleep the day he or she left Max out in the rain had seen my notices, but declined to claim Max because—as I learned too quickly—there was one critical area in which Max was anything but gentlemanly: he was not housebroken!

So now I was training *two* dogs, the springer spaniel I was boarding and Max.

Max was wonderful. Within a week, those sad eyes developed a mischievous sparkle. He also made a noise that to others probably sounded like a mere snort, but *I* could tell he was laughing. So could my son. Max was smart, too. Not all dogs are, and not all are easy to train, but Max was. With only two weeks of intensive, appropriate handling, Max became about as perfect as a pet can get.

No, I didn't keep him (even for a dog lover like me, thirteen dogs would have been absurd). With no trouble at all, I found a wonderful home for him nearby. Every now and then over the remaining years that my son and I lived in that house we'd run into Max with one of his new family's human members, which always delighted all of us.

I still sometimes wonder about his original owner. I know that someone made a heartbreaking choice to leave him outside a supermarket in the rain rather than deliver him to the local pound, in hopes that he would have a better chance of finding a home. But the odds against him being picked up by a professional dog trainer are incalculable. Most unhousebroken dogs aren't that lucky. Although sometimes, in desperation, dog owners bring in professional trainers to deal with a housebreaking problem exclusively, most tend to assume the problem is intrinsic to the dog, and give up.

This really isn't fair. Granted, some dogs are harder to train than others, but the bottom line remains the same: with the exception of incontinence grounded in medical problems, every dog *can* be housebroken! The real problem is lack of correct information or lack of disciplined consistency on the part of the owner. Lots of information is available on this subject, but dog trainers have "tricks of the trade," many of which I have never seen in print before I wrote this book. In addition, I have been training dogs for more than twenty years, during which I have developed my own Three-Step Program, incorporating these tricks into a broad, integrated process. If you follow my program, you absolutely can housebreak your dog. Even if you feel you've already been at it forever, the truth is, you haven't really begun until you institute the correct methods.

This book will help you understand the relevant aspects of dog psychology and how to make them work for you. You also will know what to expect at different ages. For example, a three-month-old puppy *cannot* go overnight without elimination; a five-month-old puppy can wait until morning. Also certain foods can decrease—or increase—a dog's need to be walked.

My Three-Step Program for successful housebreaking includes

1. proper feeding (*what* and *when* to feed),
2. cleaning to eliminate *all* odors (imperative, to keep your dog from returning to the scene of his last mess next time he has to eliminate), and
3. training methods, including conditioning techniques.

You'll also find solutions for special problems in Chapter 9, including those particular to older dogs and toy breeds. Somewhere in these pages, you'll definitely find *your* dog. I've got all of mine here; the ones I've owned, and all my "foster children"—dogs I've trained over the years.

How to Use This Book

To get the most out of this book, read all of it. The overview will strengthen your understanding of all components and how they connect with each other. Then, when you've finished, return to whichever sections seem most relevant for your immediate needs. For example, perhaps you're already feeding your dog properly but did not realize that your cleaning is inadequate. If so, move directly to the information on cleaning.

He, She, Him, and Her!

Throughout this book, I will refer to dogs as "he," with no disrespect intended toward their female counterparts. It's merely easier to stick with one sex rather than to say "he or she" every time a reference is made.

1

Common Canine Characteristics— Understanding Dogs

The Problem

This book focuses on only one issue: housebreaking. House-breaking means breaking your dog's habit of eliminating in the house. Countless dogs who end up in shelters were abandoned by their owners because they were not housebroken. Housebreaking also is the single most common problem that owners discuss, often desperately, with veterinarians.

Jimmy McCallister was a skinny, lonely, awkward, hyperactive, freckle-faced eight-year-old boy whom I met through a referral by a local veterinarian. Jimmy told me in considerable detail about his closest friend, a golden brown mixed-breed dog named Amber that had been killed by a car approximately two months earlier. In a voice stretched thin from too many tears, he concluded, "She was the only one who never got mad at me." His mother said Jimmy still slept with Amber's collar under his pillow. However, it was obvious to anyone looking even marginally below the surface that Jimmy's new floppy-eared brown-and-white canine companion, Freckles, that his parents had brought home for him six weeks earlier, already had carved her own place in his affections.

"I'm desperate!" his mother confided to me, as soon as we were alone. "He still misses Amber, but he's already so attached to Freckles—if we got rid of her, it would be like losing Amber all over again. But we're beginning to believe she cannot be housebroken. Please don't misunderstand," she added quickly. "We love our son, he needs the dog—this dog—and if that means we have to live in a house that smells like a kennel . . ."

"You don't." I assured her. "Trust me!"

It was a promise I don't usually make on the spot, but in this case I already knew from the vet who had made the referral that the dog was physically healthy.

In this, as in the vast majority of cases, the problem was not the dog. Barring medically based incontinence, failure to housebreak always stems from two factors:

1. a lack of clear, accurate, and comprehensive information
2. a lack of personal discipline in the owner, especially during the critically important early stages

Who Are the Unhousebroken?

Whether you have a young pup having several accidents a day or an adult with one accident per month, both are unhousebroken. My Three-Step Program as outlined in the next chapter and discussed in detail in Chapters 4 through

8, will guide you through successful housebreaking. First, let's lay some groundwork for understanding our goals and our pets.

Tough Love

For more than twenty years, I have been a professional dog breeder and trainer—an often exhausting, but far more often rewarding way to make a living. I love dogs, but love isn't always a soft emotion. Sometimes it needs to be tough, and this is the core of this book: *tough love*. If you're not tough and your dog does not become fully housebroken, even if you keep him, there will always be stress in your relationship. You won't understand why your pet is so stubborn or stupid or contrary or hostile, or whatever other conclusion you reach, and your dog will never understand why you are loving one moment and yet—*in the dog's perception*—so unpredictably angry the next. In short, the *quality* of your relationship will suffer.

Or, if you don't keep the pet, the odds are astronomical that the next owner, who will learn very quickly what the problem is before he or she is as attached to the dog as you were, will return it to a shelter.

Willingness to be lovingly tough is your square marked "GO," in housebreaking any dog. Your next step is learning *how*.

Misinformation Is Common—and Dangerous!

Probably the worst misinformation still floating around is that to housebreak a dog, you should rub his nose in the mess, swat him with a newspaper, then take him outside. With this process, in reality all you're really teaching is that sometimes you don't like him very much, and newspapers are frightening.

Proper Housebreaking Is Not Complicated

Initially, appropriate housebreaking can seem considerably more complicated than it really is, which is why I have broken the process down into three clear, distinct steps. My Three-Step Program incorporates a number of "tricks of the trade" that professional dog trainers often use to speed up their results. But there's no reason why you can't use them too. This "insider's guide" to housebreaking *any* dog includes many tips from top professional trainers that make them well worth the cost of their services.

Whether you are training a new puppy, or retraining an older animal, the following information on dog behavior will apply.

Understanding Dog Psychology

To housebreak a dog, it's imperative that you understand what you're dealing with. As human as they so often seem to us, dogs are *not* furry people! There is such a thing as dog psychology, and once you have a handle on it, it can become one of your most powerful tools.

First, you're smarter than your dog. Although at times you may question this fact and even feel you're locked into a war of wills with an equal—you're not. Dogs operate from instinct, not spite. Although domesticated, it's critical to remember that in their souls—and instincts—dogs are wolves. As such, they present a number of wolf-based traits that understandably displease humans. Some examples are leg lifting, howling, digging, and using urine and feces to mark their territories—with an animal frequently returning to one spot.

All canines are pack animals. This means they instinctively run in groups or "packs." Pack animals cooperate with their pack members and obey the leader. The leader defines what is expected of any dog, and trains him to obey. Thus, the key to training your dog is to set *yourself* up as the leader. This also is the key to all effective obedience training.

Obedience training will build the necessary communication skills between you and your dog that will enable him to understand what you want. An especially important element in dog psychology is the fact that *he wants to please you.* Obedience follows! The two main elements in developing a well-disciplined, healthy, happy, and housebroken dog are

1. consistency
2. patience

The Three-Step Program will teach you not only how to initially housebreak your pet, but also how to ensure his continued good behavior.

How Dogs Differ

Tiggy—short for Antigone—is a ten-month-old, female, black miniature poodle. I first met her around six o'clock on a mellow spring evening. She smiled shyly, while piddling on the recently installed wall-to-wall living room carpet in the Kalellis house, in Astoria, Queens. I had been called in to discuss a severe housebreaking problem. Also present was Mr. Kalellis's soft-spoken wife of fifteen years and two children, ages nine and twelve, all of whom obviously loved the dog.

Immediately, I realized that Tiggy was a high-strung, sensitive animal. Her piddling was a classic sign of submission, merely her instinctive language for saying, "Hey, whoever you are, you're the boss!"

To her owners, however, piddling was simply piddling. It needed to be stopped and, of course, they were right.

I have a standard list of questions I always ask on a first visit, so the four of us sat down and started talking. About five minutes into the discussion, the front door slammed with such force that—to me—it seemed as though the whole house shook. Seconds later, Nicholas Kalellis entered the living room, full of booming-loud greetings and bear hugs for his family. "Where's Tiggy?" he demanded, probably planning a final overwhelming hug for the canine member of his clan. Immediately, Tiggy performed an astonishing feat. She collapsed her own bones until she was flat enough to skittle under the couch, which is precisely what she did. (I have to confess, my own immediate instinct was to follow her.)

Now I had a solid handle on this particular problem!

Aside from the fact that *all* dogs have hearing that is considerably more acute than human hearing, different dogs also have extremely different temperaments. In Tiggy's case, the primary issue was not her undisciplined piddling; the piddling was merely a symptom. The basic problem was that she was afraid! Tiggy's owners did not understand this any more than Tiggy understood her owners; both needed to improve their communication with each other. Therefore, I made a condition. If they wanted me to, I would agree to train their pet but only if Mr. Kalellis would either lower his voice or possibly consider trading in Tiggy for a St. Bernard! What will startle and quite properly correct one dog is often entirely too much—or too little—for another. In this family, a St. Bernard's temperament would have been absolutely perfect.

A further example illustrating another aspect of this same issue—differences among individual dogs—was a wonderful golden retriever named Suspect whose owner was a cop and not one I would argue with if he ever decided to give me a ticket. His attitude and personality were part of the dog-training problem. In his view, the world consisted of good guys and bad guys, living side-by-side with good dogs and bad dogs. Good dogs did not mess on your carpet. His previous golden retriever—whose death he still mourned, although he tried not to show how much—had been fully housebroken right on schedule. Suspect, however, required a month longer, and a much stricter regimen. That was all! The point is, despite their basic common characteristics, *all* dogs—*even dogs of the same breed*—are different from each other.

Temperament is only one issue. Some dogs are easy to train, while others require considerably more patience and perseverance. Although a good deal depends on the breed as well as the individual, specific conditions of a dog's early infancy also contribute to the ease or difficulty of each case. For example, *most* dogs will not sit in their own dirt, but some will. Especially if your pup has been shut up for long periods in his sleeping quarters, he will have formed the habit of relieving himself wherever he happens to be. Therefore, the longer he has lived in a cage, the harder it will be to train him. But once again, the dog's natural instincts work in your favor; the instinct to be clean is innate to all dogs. In cases where this instinct has receded, your job, quite simply stated, is to bring it out again.

Factors Affecting Training Ease

Any dog that comes into your home brings with him an individual history. This history will affect the ease with which you'll be able to housebreak him. The bottom line, of course, is finding the dog that's right for you, no matter where he comes from, and adapting your training techniques and expectations to suit your chosen pet. However, the following are valid considerations in making that choice.

Ideal History	Less Desirable History
• Private breeder	• Pet shop
• Placement in home by the age of twelve weeks	• Confinement in a pen beyond twelve weeks
• Sedentary breed	• Active breed
• Even, sound temperament	• Nervous, sensitive, or dominant temperament

Ideal Conditions	Less Desirable Conditions
• House with a yard	• High-rise apartment
• Owner home during day	• Owner works all day
• Early introduction to the outdoors	• Late introduction to the outdoors
• Housebreaking begun in mild weather	• Housebreaking begun in rough weather

Or, if you are seeking a "previously owned" pet, the "History" list continues as follows:

• Loving private home (with children, if you have children)	• Abused or confined in a shelter for a long time
• Lived outdoors or indoors with previous owner, whichever matches your situation	• Lived outdoors or indoors with previous owner, whichever *mismatches* your situation

Additional Factors

Advice from well-intentioned but sometimes sorely misinformed friends perpetuating erroneous myths may confuse you and your pet. If you switch strategies, looking for instant results, you lose consistency and further confuse your pet.

It's also important to realize that what worked for someone else's pet may not work for yours. In addition, you may find that although you've trained previous pets, *you* are older now and possibly less patient. Or even if all general conditions are favorable, you may have wound up with a dog who simply is more difficult than most others.

Toy breeds (under twenty pounds) can be particularly difficult, which is why I've included much more on this subject in Chapter 9, "Solutions for Special Problems."

But—take heart; you *can* succeed with *your* dog!

2

An Overview of the Three-Step Program for Happy Housebreaking

Be Patient—His Life Depends on It!

Your success in housebreaking your pup and how quickly you accomplish it will depend very much on how consistently you follow the Three-Step Program, introduced here and developed in detail in Chapters 4 through 8. Although at times you may feel discouraged by the quantity of details you will need to remember, and drained by how much work is required, your dog is worth it! To housebreak him is one of the most loving gifts you will ever give him. Without it, he probably will not live a long or happy life—with you or anyone else.

Also, it may help to keep in mind that the labor-intensive early stage is temporary. The time spent learning your dog's personality and body needs is necessary only during the early months of his life. In the vast majority of cases, getting training right the first time means you do it only once. Occasionally you may run into an unusual circumstance when you will have to remind him of the good habits you have already instilled in him, but this is a short-term project.

The Three-Step Program

The Three-Step Program is a distillation of my twenty years' experience as a professional dog trainer. It works! Follow it thoroughly and accurately and for as long as your pet lives with you, you will have a well-behaved animal you can be proud of, enjoy, and take on visits to family and friends. In addition, if for any reason you someday must give him up, your odds on finding him a good home elsewhere go way up!

The three steps are

1. Appropriate *Feeding*
2. Thorough *Cleaning*
3. Diligent *Training*

All are interrelated, and each is equally important for success.

Step One—Appropriate FEEDING

What and *when* you feed your dog are the components of Step One of the Three-Step Program. As surprising as this may sound, with the right food your dog's need to eliminate will drop from five to three or possibly even two times a day. In addition, his stools will be firmer and, thus, easier for you to clean.

I recommend quality or premium dry food only. Over the last fifteen years, new lines of quality dry foods or kibble that contain more meat than grain have become available in pet stores and in some supermarkets. These foods are superior to most of the common supermarket brands because:

1. They reduce how often your dog will need to eliminate, and because more of the food is actually assimilated, quality brands produce fewer stools.
2. Meat produces firmer stools, which makes cleanup considerably easier!
3. The meat content makes them taste better, thus allowing the finicky dog to enjoy dry kibble.
4. They provide complete nutrition; no supplements are required.
5. They contain 5–10 percent more fat; fat helps maintain your dog's weight, and keeps his coat shiny.

Moist food—either packaged or canned—is necessary only if your pup is extraordinarily finicky and absolutely will not eat anything else.

For more detailed information on feeding, see Chapter 4.

Does any of this mean you will *never* be able to share your own food with your pet? Not at all! Later, once your dog is *thoroughly* housebroken, if the mood strikes both dog and owner, by all means pass on your table scraps, and occasionally vary his standard diet.

But—until housebreaking is complete—the love that motivates us to please him, to enjoy it when he wags his tail in delight, is not enough. The tough love described in Chapter 1 means choosing a food and a schedule and sticking to them!

Step Two—Thorough CLEANING

Sarah Bernstein owned a rather serious, six-year-old, house-broken, male beagle that she actually named "Fang." As much as she loved him, she also considered him an important security measure: a watchdog for an attractive single woman in her early thirties living alone in New York City. For many years she had survived an uneasy truce with a landlord any tenant could easily hate, so naturally she was delighted when she finally found an apartment in a building in which the landlord accepted tenants who owned dogs. In fact, on the day she checked it out, it warmed her heart merely to walk through the halls and hear herself barked at by an assortment of conscientious canines, all alerting either their owners or merely other dogs to the fact that a mysterious human being was afoot.

Three weeks later, the present tenants—a young married couple with a mixed-breed dog—moved out.

The apartment included lovely carpeting and drapes, and gave off that clean, fresh paint smell.

However, the next morning Sarah awoke to an astonishing gift from Fang—a dark stain on the side of her couch, ending in a puddle on the floor. Because she had had absolutely no soiling problems with him since he was a pup, she attributed it to nervousness in his new environment. She quite firmly told him, "No," then thoroughly scrubbed the offending area for half an hour, using her strongest household cleaner. Believing the accident to be a fluke, she simply went on with her life. Two days later—surprise!—he did it again, this time on the drapes!

Two weeks later, I got a phone call. That morning, Fang had redecorated the couch *and* the drapes! No, he wasn't sick, and as far as she could tell, he had settled in very nicely—except that he continued to mess, by now throughout the whole apartment.

After determining that the previous tenants also had owned a dog, I asked her what I always ask in these circumstances: were there any stains, any indication at all, that the previous dog might not have been fully housebroken?

"Absolutely not," she assured me. "In fact," she insisted, "it's one of the cleanest apartments I've ever seen. Remember last week, when it rained? And you know how dampness brings out odors? There weren't any. I'm positive."

So I visited her—and brought my black-fluorescent light, an instrument for revealing urine stains invisible to the naked eye. Although I describe this tool in more detail in Chapter 5, in most cases, you don't really need it. In most cases, *I* don't need it, but in this one I doubted whether there was any other way the client would believe me.

I turned off the lights and turned on the black-fluorescent light. Together we discovered glowing evidence of the previous tenants' dog's indiscretions throughout the apartment. Sarah was astonished at the quantity.

Now, she realized, she had two options; either thoroughly clean and *neutralize* the rug, or replace it. A neutralizer is a substance that shields the odor so that neither you *nor your dog* can smell it. However, this initial effect wears off, through time and foot traffic. Neutralizers must be patiently, repeatedly applied, until enough soaks into the carpet and padding to thoroughly destroy the odor. In most cases, neutralizers are necessary, unless you are cleaning a *nonporous* (usually relatively new linoleum or tile) floor. For more on this and on effective cleaners and neutralizers you can create yourself at a fraction of what their commercially-prepared counterparts cost, see Chapter 5.

Because Sarah didn't really care for the rug's color, she decided to replace it, but this was strictly a matter of choice. In less than two weeks of tight supervision and, when necessary, confinement, Fang was once again her beloved friend and defender, with no more housebreaking difficulties.

Keeping your living quarters free from the scent of *any* pet's waste is imperative when originally housebreaking, and also to prevent relapses. Although to you, a carpet may appear and even smell clean, a dog's sensitive nose, being one to ten thousand times more acute than a human's, can smell even one drop of urine in any room, and dogs instinctively return to any spot on which they detect even the faintest scent of urine or feces. Thus, inadequate cleaning and neutralizing encourages a repeat of earlier transgressions.

Step Three—Diligent TRAINING

Good communication between pet and owner is critical to the success of any type of animal training. To establish this communication, your pup must trust you. Consistency in how you handle him builds trust, giving him clarity in his efforts to learn which actions warrant praise and which evoke a correction. This understanding gives him the emotional security of knowing what is and isn't acceptable to you. Remember, a properly-trained dog not only loves you, he also *respects* you, as leader of his pack. Be patient! Patience will make his training considerably less stressful for both of you, especially if you happen to have wound up with a pup who is a little slow in understanding what you want.

However, depending on your particular situation, communication with your *dog* is not always the only issue. The O'Malley household on Long Island consisted of six children ranging in age from eight through seventeen, two parents, one grandmother, a cat, and a hamster. Except for the cat and hamster, all cheerfully agreed to walk Lady, their cocker spaniel pup. The problem was, they never quite got around to making up *and writing down* a schedule clearly defining which person would be responsible for which walks. Ironically, the arguments over who should clean up, mess by mess, collectively took more time than would have been necessary to walk her, because, of course, a walk would have required only one human participant.

In summary, communication, a feeding and walking schedule, and cooperation from *all* two- and four-footed members of the household are imperative for successful training.

Dog Owners—Then and Now

Years ago, most dog owners were families living in houses with yards, and a full-time parent at home. Today, far more dog owners are apartment-dwelling, working singles, like Sarah, or apartment-dwelling, working couples, like her predecessors. *The training principles laid out in this book respect the fact that your time with your new pet may be limited.* In fact, today, whether pets live in apartments or houses, most are alone most of the time. Sometimes you can be with them every moment, watching for accidents, cleaning immediately, but sometimes you simply can't. This book will show you how to make the most of what time you *do* have to actively train your pup.

In Chapters 3 and 6 through 9, you'll find training tools and guidelines. If at first glance this part of the process seems discouragingly time-consuming, remember that most of it is *temporary*, while the results—a housebroken dog—are permanent!

Health

Before beginning the Three-Step Program, it is imperative to make sure your dog is healthy. He should have good weight, a shiny coat, clear eyes, a healthy appetite, and firm stools. A good veterinarian will make an assessment during the first visit. It is critically important that he or she check a stool sample to make sure your pet is free of intestinal parasites (worms), which cause soft and more frequent stools. *Pups with worms cannot be trained* because they cannot control their stool. Worms are contracted by sniffing an infected stool, and pups continue to be most susceptible to contracting worms during their first six months.

Nor are worms your only concern. Numerous other health disorders can be transmitted during this early, vulnerable period, which is why it's important to keep him indoors until his first series of shots is complete, usually by the age of three months.

Rawhide Toys and Health

In Chapter 3, "Tools of the Trade," supplies are discussed. One is rawhide toys. Whether or not you allow your dog to have rawhide chew toys is a decision you must make in conjunction with your vet. Some vets disapprove of them, because occasionally a pup's stomach will be upset by whatever rawhide residue he swallows. This upset may affect his stools and therefore his ability to be housebroken. However, I have found this to be a problem in only a small percentage of cases. I believe the toys are helpful as a training tool because during housebreaking there will be times when the dog must be restricted to a limited area (confined); the rawhide toys will keep him occupied, thus making this a less negative experience. Therefore if your vet—and, of course, your dog's reaction—indicate no objections, I strongly recommend them.

3

Tools of the Trade

Assemble Tools in Advance

Like many other loving parents throughout the world, Carlos Gomez brought home a puppy—a sparkle-eyed, fluffy little Pomeranian that pretty much fit into the palm of his hand—to surprise and delight his two young daughters on Christmas Eve. He also bought a couple of cans of dog food at the corner grocery store, had saved two days' newspapers, and already had decided that just for that night the pup could sleep in his daughters' room. The rest, he and his wife had agreed earlier, could be taken care of later. Right?

Wrong! In fact, as the Gomez family promptly discovered when they awoke to a surprising quantity of calling cards from their four-legged newest family member, an unhousebroken cuddly canine even of that size can, indeed, make you absolutely nuts!

Proper housebreaking begins the moment you carry your pup across your threshold, and this means you must be fully prepared *in advance.* Anything less is naive and unfair to your pet. Obviously, when you stop to think about it, it makes sense that instilling good habits from the beginning will be easier than overcoming bad ones later. And habits in a new environment can develop quickly.

Therefore, get ready, get set—before you pick up the dog!

Not every item discussed in this chapter is necessary in every case. For example, if you have a toy breed that will be living in your apartment, obviously you do not need a dog house! However, certain other items require choices considerably less apparent. For example, although crates can be helpful, they have certain drawbacks and are not necessary. The decision is yours.

Indoors

Crates—Yes or No?

A crate utilizes the principle that a dog will not willingly sit in its own mess. Thus, confining him to a very limited area will encourage him to hold his urine and feces until he can be brought to an appropriate elimination site.

Crates should never, under any circumstances, be used for a very young pup who has little control. The only message using a crate too soon will give your pup is that you do want him to sit in his own dirt, because you are giving him no choice!

A crate is a cage made of wire, open on all sides. I do not recommend plastic carrying cases, because they are not nearly as open as crates. Crates are definitely preferable: your dog will feel considerably less isolated. A crate should be approximately the length of your dog and high enough to allow him to stand and turn around, but no larger. If it is too large, it must be partitioned off to prevent him from dirtying one end then simply sitting at the other. Place his bed inside. *Never use newspapers for his bed.*

After training is complete, with the door left open the crate itself can be used as a bed.

Though crates have become quite popular during the last decade and are a convenient tool, sometimes they are overused; they prevent accidents, but the real training is accomplished elsewhere. To be effective as a training tool, crates must be part of a rigid schedule—crate time, outdoor time, indoor play time. Such a regular schedule may not always be possible for a family to maintain. In addition, crates range in price from around fifty dollars to more than a hundred dollars, while less expensive methods of confinement can be equally effective. The following example uses a short leash to confine the dog and effect training.

Marlene Carter, a divorced working mother of two school-age boys, Brandon and Vince, was constantly struggling to find reliable baby-sitters, but baby-sitters also willing and able to keep up with her five-month-old Doberman were rare. More often than not, the baby-sitter simply put Pepper out into the fenced-in backyard, sometimes with a sweater, sometimes not. Dobermans are short-haired and hate cold weather, and Pepper was particularly good at looking heartbreakingly pathetic. Result? Someone always let him back inside, after which, without exception, he promptly relieved himself, usually on the living room or dining room carpet.

In early December, Marlene called me.

Under no circumstances does the "tough love" necessary to train your pet ever include inflicting physical pain on him—and freezing is painful! Instead, after I had collected all the necessary information, the goal on which Marlene and I focused was to induce Pepper to eliminate *as soon as he got outside.*

With this in mind, we rigged up a short leash attached to the baseboard with a screw-in hook, in a small hallway area where he would have to sit in any mess he created. We then drew up a schedule whereby he would be let outside for a few minutes only at certain preestablished times that had been coordinated with his feeding schedule.

Now his choices were considerably more limited. He could eliminate as soon as he was let out; if he did not he would be brought back in and tied with the short leash where eventually he would have to sit in his own mess.

Within five days, Pepper made the decision always to eliminate as soon as he was let out. All this was years ago and because Marlene and I became and have remained good friends, I know he hasn't had a single accident since, even during cold weather!

"Throw Cans" Help Deter Indoor Accidents

A "throw can" is the ultimate housebreaking weapon. It is an aluminum soda can filled with about ten pennies, with a piece of tape covering the opening. *Keep several within easy reach, anywhere your pup may wander throughout your living quarters.* Toss a throw can at his feet if he starts to eliminate indoors. The noise from the can is startling and makes an impressive correction. He will scamper off, his accident interrupted, and thus he will retain something to deposit out-side—so take him out *immediately*. Also, throw cans will enable you to catch transgressions more quickly and from far-ther away. The can is especially helpful if you are by nature soft-spoken.

If your floors are hard—wood or tile—or if your dog is high-strung, wrap a cloth around the can to cushion the sound. Conversely, a giant or more sedate breed may need a larger can or more pennies to get his attention.

Incidentally, if you're feeling creative, wrapping the cans with preglued shelf- or wallpaper can turn them into whim-sical accents for any room's decor. Perhaps you'd prefer to decorate for a particular season, holiday, or whatever else appeals to you.

Gates

Initially it will be necessary to confine your new pup to a specific area in the house—one room or possibly a hallway. This is not the same as confining him to an extremely lim-ited area, as was the case with Marlene's Doberman. The goal of this kind of confinement is merely to keep him *where you can see him*, so that other housebreaking principles may be utilized. For this, you will need an accordion or mesh gate so he can see out and not feel isolated. (Be careful with an accordion gate; if he's small enough, he may get his head caught in it.)

Here, again, tough love is important. The sooner you start using the right tools—even when they make him temporar-ily unhappy—the sooner you'll be able to allow him the complete freedom both of you want. The gate will keep him from wandering the house. Sometimes he'll be confined to another room where he can see you but cannot be with you. You, however, can observe his actions to note when he needs to go out. The more reinforcement he gets for eliminating outdoors, the sooner you'll be able to give him the run of the house.

About Beds

Dogs are "denning" creatures (they like dens, caves, and similar defined small spaces). Your pet's own bed will help him feel secure. If you use a crate, it's kindest to put his bed inside; he'll be more comfortable. Also, while housebreaking him, you'll have plenty of cleaning to do; you don't need the added burden of excessive pet hair all over the place! Pups that rest in their own beds considerably reduce this problem.

Beds come in a wide variety of sizes, materials, and fillers. Mats are convenient for large breeds and some mats have removable covers that can be washed. Avoid beds with sides or wicker frames if your particular pup tends to chew anything he can get his teeth on. Tying a toy to his bed can help distract him from other mischief.

Indoor Keep-It-Clean Supplies

Make sure you have these supplies on hand:

1. white vinegar
2. baking soda
3. paper towels and/or rags
4. sponges

5. *ammonia-free* household cleaner
6. a spray bottle
7. rubber gloves

You will learn in Chapter 5 how to use these items for thorough cleaning.

However, if you anticipate that the odors created by these cleaners may offend you, or that your dog may require stronger measures, then pick up some commercially-prepared cleaners and neutralizers, available at your local pet store. The most popular today seem to be Nature's Miracle and Nil Odor, but others may be equally effective.

Repellents

If all else fails—if despite all your best efforts your pup still returns to the same spot over and over—probably you'll need a repellent. A repellent is a substance to be used on the offending area which will send him skittering away by leaving an odor he will hate even more than he loves the odor he created the last time he visited that particular spot. Homemade repellents such as undiluted vinegar, air fresheners, disinfectants, and perfumes may be sufficient. If your repellent doesn't do the job, your pet store will have commercial preparations.

Collars and Leashes

As with Marlene's Doberman, a collar and leash can be used as a crate substitute. This is not, however, their primary purpose. Any time you catch your pet in an accident, getting him outside *fast* is critical. If a collar and sometimes a leash already are on him, getting him outdoors in time to finish in a designated area rather than on the way to your door is much easier. *Avoid leashes made of chains!* They are hard on both your pup and your hands. In addition, he can seriously injure himself if he gets tangled up in one. Simple canvas or nylon leads are best and also are the least expensive. Always use a buckle collar or harness of canvas, nylon, or leather. No chokers, please, for very young pups.

Outdoors

Restraining Equipment

Cold Weather Comfort Tip: use a retractable leash to let your pup get to his outdoor spot while you remain at the doorway.

When using a tie-out system (see next paragraph), use a buckle collar or halter. Never use a choke collar.

Tie-Out Systems

If you have a yard or other area around your house that is not fenced-in, a tie-out system will allow your pet to spend time outside without you being present to monitor his whereabouts. Tie-out systems are long lines with snaps on both ends. They come in cable, nylon, canvas, or chain (I do not recommend chain). They also come in a variety of sizes, fold up or retractable, anchored to a wall or attached to a stake in the ground, or running overhead with a trolley system. Be sure he has plenty of clean water in a cool, shaded area; you don't need to be concerned with his urination outside. However, be sure to remove the water at least one hour before you bring him inside.

Helpful Strictly Outside Supplies

Although none of these is essential, all are valuable investments.

1. Yard scoops come in a variety of sizes, and make the job of cleaning outside waste practically painless.
2. Yard deodorizers (commercially prepared, available in pet shops) are powerful cleaners for outside problem areas, where elimination odors, especially on concrete, can become overwhelming.
3. Dog stool disposal systems are miniature septic systems and enable you to dispose of whatever needs to be disposed of, into the ground.

Dog Coats

Dog sweaters and coats are good in cold weather for toy and short-haired breeds. When it rains, all breeds can benefit from the extra protection of a dog raincoat. In addition, in the early stages of housebreaking you'll be taking your pup out a lot and a raincoat will spare you the added burden of drying your wet pooch—again and again! It's also a good idea to practice putting the coat onto your dog several times when not going out, to accustom him to the coat and to train him not to chew it.

Indoors and Out

Toys

Balls, rawhide bones, and things that go squeak—never underestimate the value of toys in your pet's life! In addition, you're off to a much better start if you give him something you know he likes to keep him amused when you're not available for play or even to keep him company. Use bins or laundry baskets to store toys; one for outdoors and a second for indoors (to avoid dragging outside dirt onto your carpets). In fact, some pups enjoy emptying and refilling these bins, a harmless occupation when they are home alone. Never give as a toy anything overly similar to something you value, such as old shoes or discarded stuffed animals. Your pup cannot distinguish between these and the shoes or whatever else you still value! Also, remember to check with your vet before incorporating anything made of rawhide to avoid digestion problems. Beware of anything that might break and choke your puppy, or anything that might splinter or be toxic.

Dishes 'n' Such

You'll find no shortage of selections; keep in mind that his dishes need to be reasonably stable, not easily tipped over by eager little paws stomping through dinner. Timed feeders are convenient for busy owners, and water bottles can pacify a thirsty pup when his housebreaking schedule prohibits the quantity of liquid he'd really prefer. Heated bowls are available to prevent water from freezing outdoors.

To keep bugs out of his food outdoors, simply place his food bowl in the center of a larger dish and pour water into the larger dish. Any invaders will be done in by the moat. Or, if you feel like splurging, you now can buy a bowl designed on this principle.

Ready, Get Set . . .

At last, you're almost ready to bring him home. You still need something on hand to feed him and a clearly spelled-out schedule on when to feed. Both needs will be dealt with in Chapter 4.

4

Step One—Feeding

While Housebreaking, No Snacks and No People Food!

Amy Clark, a red-headed, energetic, nine-year-old tomboy, hated vegetables. It was a subject on which, for many years, she had been locked into a war-of-wills with her mother. Then—magically—one day she apparently began finishing everything green, yellow, and even red on her plate.

Unfortunately, only Amy noticed that the clean plates coincided with the arrival of Sparky, a delightful and well-named, seven-month-old, flop-eared, mixed-breed pup. The problem was, despite the entire family's responsible and disciplined efforts to housebreak Sparky, he remained unpredictable, especially in failing to hold overnight. With two kids and with both parents working long hours, Mr. and Mrs. Clark were so overwhelmed that finally they seriously considered giving up the dog.

Sometimes when diagnosing an individual problem, dog trainers must play Sherlock Holmes, and sometimes it takes a while—but not in this case! As much as I hated ratting on Amy, it was the lesser of two evils. From my first visit it was apparent that Amy and Sparky shared an extraordinary emotional bond that far transcended the short-range advantages to Amy of using Sparky as a canine automatic vegetable-disposal unit!

What Amy did not understand is that what and when a dog is fed greatly affects housebreaking. Without control in these two critical areas—which Amy was giving up in relation to Sparky not only at dinner but also in lovingly sharing her after-school potato chips and candy—any dog becomes subject to unpredictable elimination. This, in turn, creates a need for more walks than otherwise would be necessary.

Control His Eating, Control His Elimination Time Frame!

Remember, everything that goes into your pup's belly will be processed through his digestive system within a specific time frame influenced every bit as much by when as by what he has eaten. Understanding this is critically important if you are to establish an effective schedule for walking him.

A schedule is critical; tightly controlled rules on what and when you feed your pup will determine when walks will be necessary. You must create a schedule, then follow it with patience and consistency. The schedule assures that you will be able to walk your puppy when he *needs* to go out.

No Dawdling Over Dinner!

Because *when* your pup eats is so important in determining a successful schedule for walks, make his food and water available to him for no more than fifteen minutes per feeding. Food available indefinitely can be nibbled at indefinitely, which leaves you guessing—indefinitely—on when to take him out. Restricting his food is not unkind. Remember, dogs are wolves. Their nature is to forage for food, eating when it becomes available. Your pup is *not* suffering because he can't raid the refrigerator. Leaving food and water down all day will make it impossible for you to predict or regulate his elimination schedule. If you are going to housebreak in any reasonable length of time without suffering a nervous breakdown, both food and water need to be offered only within predetermined time frames.

If, after the full fifteen minutes he still hasn't finished, probably one of the following reasons will explain why:

1. He's been previously conditioned to having food always available.
2. You're offering him too much.
3. His attention is being diverted.
4. He *really* doesn't like his food!

Reprogramming Bad Habits

If he's already established the habit of munching and drinking whenever the spirit moves him because the food and water have been constantly available, select a time when you'll be home all day, and take away both his food and water, then put them down again only for preset intervals. Thus, you will prepare him for being without them next time you must be away without the transition being too jarring.

Only after the housebreaking is complete, will you make water available all the time.

Double-Check "Available" Water Supply

What water is "available" may surprise you! Ying was one of those extraordinarily beautiful mutts that nature occasionally creates, once only, never to duplicate. Part chow and the rest God-only-knows-what, at age six months Ying was encouragingly predictable and 100 percent trained on solid elimination. However his wetting—here, there, and everywhere—was overwhelming. His owners, Ling and Lee Sung, both worked long hours as computer professionals and already had managed to acquire a large mortgage on a sparsely-furnished house with a convenient fenced-in backyard.

I first met them on a cold, drizzly Saturday afternoon in late January, unfit weather for most dogs and definitely unfit for this particular dog trainer to be outside for any length of time.

"Every morning, as soon as we get up, we let Ying out into the backyard," Ling told me, nodding towards the sliding glass doors which showed a winter-barren but obviously well-landscaped outside area. Throughout the conversation, Lee sat on the floor playing with Ying who wagged, wiggled, and nuzzled, obviously delighted with the attention. "And he does urinate," Ling continued. "I've watched him. Then we feed him, let him out again and take up his water dish before we leave for work. At 2:00 P.M. our neighbor comes in, gives him food and water, then lets him out again an hour later. And I believe her that he goes, but when he comes back in, he keeps wetting all over the place. We don't want to leave him outside all day in this weather, but . . ." Her glance encompassed the damage she had showed me in great detail when I arrived, followed by, "We want him, we love him, but most of this isn't even paid for!"

My eyes did a fast search, quickly locating the available water culprits from similar circumstances with more than one previous client. First I looked through the glass doors at about half a dozen empty flowerpots filled with rainwater. Then I asked, "Where's your bathroom?"

She pointed.

"Any others?"

"Well—yes. Two more upstairs."

"Mind if I look?"

Obviously with second thoughts about having allowed this peculiar person—me—into their home, they humored me. My suspicions proved to be accurate. Two of the bathroom doors were open, and both toilet lids were up. Within another couple of minutes, all of us—except the dog—were laughing. All difficulties should be this easy to resolve! First, they needed to make sure that all toilet lids were down before they went to work and, second, either Ling or Lee and, later, their neighbor, would have to actually leash and supervise Ying's backyard outings to make sure he wasn't drinking from not only the flowerpots but also from rain or melted-snow puddles in the yard. In addition, of course, they would need to clean, neutralize, and probably use a repellent on all problem areas throughout the house.

By scheduling Ying's access to water, the Lees also scheduled his need to urinate, and thus were able to complete his housebreaking.

Minimize/Eliminate Distractions

If you, the kids, the cat, the parakeet—you name it—are all in motion when you place your pup's food in front of him, and with added distractions of a phone, a radio, and a television set, even a very hungry pup may have difficulty concentrating on his food! Solution? Find a quiet corner for the allotted fifteen-minute mealtime, even if it means moving him somewhere else. If you do move him, be sure you take him to the same place every day so that his attention will not be diverted by the newness of his surroundings.

In addition, never touch him while he's eating. Adorable as he is, and as much as he needs you to express your love and approval, even a pat on his head while he's eating can be an overwhelming distraction. However, after he's finished, by all means show your affection, perhaps even with a gentle pat on his full stomach!

Feed Him What He Likes!

A key factor in establishing predictable elimination patterns is to encourage your pet to eat quickly and consistently. This is why it's important to feed him what he *likes*. You want him to be satisfied, not to pick and dawdle.

I strongly recommend only quality or premium *dry* food. In addition to its advantages in creating fewer stools, it also is more convenient than cans, and it needs to be chewed. Chewing will help minimize the plaque on his teeth.

However, finding what he likes may require trial and error experimentation. Sample packets of a variety of quality dry foods are available at most pet shops and, unlike cats, most dogs have no objection to eating the same food all the time. This means that once you've found a food that your dog likes, stick with it while housebreaking! Because different foods are digested within different time frames, sticking to only one food while you are housebreaking gives you predictability on planning his walks.

Exceptions

For the young pup (three to five months) having trouble with the dry meal because he is teething, warm water—never milk!—may be used to moisten the dry food. *Milk causes diarrhea.*

However, if—just your luck!—your particular pet turns out to be a fussy eater, try mixing something from a can with the dry meal. There are two kinds of canned food: chunks and chopped. Again, premium canned food is best. For mixing, I recommend chopped because it is easier to blend into the dry food. Start with one tablespoon and increase the amount only if needed to entice your pet to eat. Quite commonly, toy breeds require at minimum at least some moist food. In rare cases, the entire meal will have to be from either a moist packet or a can.

When making any kind of change (adding canned or moist food), gradually add the new food over a three-day period to avoid upsetting his digestion. Usually switching from one *quality* dry food to another will have no adverse effects.

Read Labels to Determine Quality of a Food

Learn to read labels. Always, the first or, at minimum, the second ingredient listed should be meat—chicken, beef, or lamb—(except in a vegetarian formula) and the fat content should be no lower than 12 percent.

In most puppy foods, the protein content is comparable and acceptable for most pups, ranging from 26 to 30 percent. However, the fat content is another story entirely, ranging all the way from 9 to 20 percent. Beware of foods with a fat content below 12 percent; usually this indicates the food is more grain than meat, which most dogs find less tasty and which will produce more stool. In addition, higher fat will help your growing pup achieve and maintain a good healthy weight. (If you are housebreaking an overweight, full-grown dog, you may need to cut *back* on fat intake, just as overweight humans also need to be careful in this area.)

The following tables provide a general comparison of pet shop brands with supermarket brands. Although pet shop brands are often superior, recently more and more quality food has been finding its way onto supermarket shelves.

Pet Shops

Brand	Protein	Fat	Main Ingredients
A	28%	17%	Chicken by-products, ground corn, rice, flour meal
B	26%	16%	Lamb, wheat flour, ground rice

Supermarkets

Brand	Protein	Fat	Main Ingredients
C	27%	9%	Ground yellow corn, corn gluten meal, brewer's rice
D	21%	8%	Corn, meat and bone meal, wheat

Storage

Store dry food in a cool place, and be careful to not over-stock during summer. In summer, bugs that are dormant in winter and thus not a problem, may surprise you with their ability to infest food you thought was perfectly free of them.

If you happen to have wound up with an extra-finicky pup who requires moist packets or canned food mixed with his dry food, it's okay to store cans in any season. In addition, you can save money if you buy cans by the case. Be sure before you buy, to check the food's shelf life.

How Long Puppy Food Should Be Used

In most cases, special puppy food should be used until your pet is approximately one year old. If you have a giant breed, it's best to stay with puppy food for a year and a half.

How Much to Feed

The eye of the master feeds his dog! Or, otherwise stated, if your pup never or rarely finishes what you give him, pay attention to how much he leaves. If he leaves a lot, probably you're offering too much. As with human beings, pups have different-size appetites, which aren't always predictable. When an occasional one or two bites—no more—remain in the dish, you've found the right amount, although this also can be affected by how much physical energy he expended on any particular day.

All dog food labels include feeding instructions regarding appropriate quantity according to the dog's age and size. If you feed him *quality* food, he will require less than with cheap brands because it is more concentrated. Like humans, your pup will require increasing amounts of food while he is growing. At maturity his food needs will stabilize.

Feeding Guidelines

Age	Meals per Day	Comments
2–3 months	3–4	Your pup usually will cut back on meals by himself
4–6 months	2–3	Eliminate a meal if he appears disinterested
6–10 months	2	You may substitute a few unflavored dog biscuits for the second meal
10–15 months	1–2	

Water per Day

Water must be included with each meal. In watering your pup, the amount does not depend on his age or size. Simply give him as much as he wants, within the allotted meal time frame. However, regardless of how many meals he eats, be sure water is available to him at least three or four times a day, with these intervals spread out over the entire day. His last water, no later than two hours before his last walk, should be no more than half as much as he normally consumes at other times. The only exception is that on hot days you may want to pacify him periodically with one or two ice cubes, depending on his size.

When to Feed

As far as your pup is concerned, you create what constitutes his "day." For example, if you worked nights, "morning" would be when you opened your eyes in the late afternoon or early evening, following a "good day's sleep." According to whatever your schedule is, figure that a "day" consists of approximately sixteen hours. Within this sixteen-hour time frame, space his meals and walks according to his age, with whatever adjustments you and your particular pup may require.

No matter what schedule eventually evolves, *never feed him late in the "evening."* This is nonnegotiable in training and maintaining a housebroken pooch. Schedule his last meal, if possible, no later than 5:00 P.M. or the equivalent according to your particular time frame, so that he can eliminate during the last walk and remain empty "overnight." If five o'clock is not feasible, then do the best you can, but keep it as early as possible.

Rawhide Bones to the Rescue!

Particularly in the beginning and sometimes even after your pet grows accustomed to the disciplined eating patterns described in this chapter, occasionally he's going to let you know he's not exactly pleased with any of it. And, unfortunately, there's no way you can explain to him that none of it is forever; all of it is merely support for a goal that actually will be reached considerably faster *with* the discipline.

However, assuming your vet and your dog's digestion have no objections, you do have the option of pacifying him with rawhide bones. Because rawhide is not food, it will not conflict with his eating schedule. Especially if you've taken food away when he was used to having it constantly available, a rawhide bone can ease the transition. Rawhide comes in several sizes and degrees of chewiness—soft for young pups, hard for large breeds. Don't overdo; keep it special, for special occasions, such as easing him out of having food constantly available, or when you are confining him in a restricted area.

When the rawhide gets old and dirty—as happens fairly quickly—get rid of it! Fresh rawhide is best.

5

Step Two—Cleaning

Thorough Cleaning Is Critical!

What looks and smells clean to *you* may not be enough to deter your pet from soiling. It's critically important to understand your pet has a superior sense of smell, and if he smells even the faintest trace of his last transgression, he will soil again in that spot.

The success of your cleaning regimen will be apparent only through your dog's behavior. If he soils again, you must take increasingly stronger measures. The good news is that there are many measures to take.

People-Clean vs. Dog-Clean

Lily Bartlett was in her mid-sixties, looked ten years younger, and had an energy level I envied. Widowed for several years, she lived with her son and daughter-in-law and cared for her adorable freckle-faced four-year-old identical twin grandsons while their parents worked. The family's ten room house was astonishingly clean, even after they acquired Droopy, a largely beagle mixed-breed female pup.

The first time I walked into the living room, I noticed the freshly vacuumed carpet and the soft scent of lemon polish on wooden furniture that gleamed in the late afternoon sunlight. Certainly no one is happy with an unhousebroken pet, but for anyone as immaculate as Lily, this had to be one of her worst nightmares.

The second time I visited, Droopy was outside and Lily was visibly upset. "She did it again, less than a minute ago," Lily told me as she started back inside from the open door. "I'm sorry the boys are so attached to her, because I am fed up. We should have named her 'Puddles.' I've done everything you told me last time, and she *still* wets all over the place!"

I followed her into the living room, then did a fast double-take when I saw her cleaning supplies on the shiny glass-topped coffee table: a bucket with water, a sponge, rubber gloves, and a bottle of ammonia-based household cleaner. Ammonia is a primary component in urine, which limits its effectiveness under these circumstances, so stick with pine or other ammonia-free cleaners!

And that was only half of it. As I sat on the couch, Lily "cleaned" the offending area, periodically wringing the sponge into the bucket, thereby contaminating the cleaning solution itself with the urine she'd just picked up, spreading it back onto the floor with each additional wipe. Certainly to Lily, when she finished, the rug was clean of Droopy's scent—but not to Droopy or to any other canine! The point is, not only what you use to clean but also how you clean are critically important.

Wkat to Use

The following cleaners are listed in incremental order, starting with the mildest preparation. If your dog is confined to a nonporous linoleum floor, any common household cleaner should be sufficient. However, if you have an odor-absorbing porous floor, or tiles with even minuscule odor-catching spaces between them, you will need to move to the next level. Whatever you use, be sure to test the area for colorfastness. Also, your hands will be in water quite a bit, sometimes with strong cleaners. *Wear rubber gloves.* In fact, keep several pairs handy!

1. Ammonia-free commercial household cleaners
2. Homemade neutralizers
3. Commercially prepared neutralizers
4. Repellents

Homemade Neutralizers

A neutralizer covers an odor as though you had placed a pane of glass over it, thus preventing your pup from detecting it. To prepare your own at a fraction of the commercial cost, combine one part vinegar with three parts water in a spray bottle. Keep it handy with a sponge to clean the area as soon as an accident occurs. On carpets, sprinkle baking soda over the offending area; it absorbs moisture as well as odors. Then clean with your vinegar-and-water solution.

Commercially Prepared Neutralizers

Commercially prepared neutralizers are available in pet stores. They may be stronger than the vinegar-and-water solution. Also, if you simply dislike the smell of the vinegar and baking soda, commercially prepared mixtures have considerably more pleasant scents.

Repellents

Repellents can be homemade or commercial. You will find their scent tolerable; your dog will not! In fact, your dog will find them so offensive, he'll avoid any place where they have been sprayed which, of course, is precisely what you want to happen. Repellents should be used to deter your pet only if he has established a favorite spot. Many dogs find scatter rugs particularly appealing.

Undiluted vinegar, pungent air fresheners, disinfectants, and perfume sometimes can be effective repellents or you may want to purchase a repellent from the pet store.

Don't Underestimate the Extent of the Problem!

As stated earlier, how you clean is just as important as what you use, but there's another aspect that needs your attention. Most people tend to underestimate the extent of the problem and therefore clean insufficiently, no matter how many products they use. Usually you'll see very quickly if a dog's feces are not all in the same place, but urine is another matter. Unfortunately, dogs have no manners in this respect. Quite cheerfully—or frantically, if you've caught them in the act and are making your displeasure clearly visible—dogs will run right through their urine, carrying the odor far from its original site. In fact, if your dog is a leg lifter, damage may extend to walls, drapes, and furniture.

In short, whether his original transgression was on a non-carpeted or carpeted surface, to keep him from returning to the same general area to relieve himself, when you clean, often you must cover a far broader area than is obvious.

How to Clean Wood, Tile, or Linoleum Floors

Start with the main mess. Pick up (if necessary), then blot the obviously offending area with paper towels or rags. Use a clean mop or sponge with the cleaner of your choice.

Be sure to clean a wide enough area to eliminate any tracked urine or odor. If you must clean a large area, use fresh cleaning solution for a second pass to keep from spreading the pet's scent with contaminated cleaner.

Carpets

To clean urine from carpets:

1. Blot
2. Sprinkle
3. Neutralize
4. Repel if necessary

Blot up as much liquid as possible with paper towels or rags. (*Do not* use a sponge which will spread the odor back into your cleaning water when you rinse it.) Then sprinkle carpet-cleaning granules or baking soda to absorb the rest. Vacuum, then neutralize. Neutralizing always should be done at least twice to reach carpet padding.

Odors can remain for quite a while—even months! *Make sure any unneutralized former problem areas are treated!*

Whether you need a repellent will be revealed to you over the next day or so by your pup's behavior. If he sniffs—and sniffs, and sniffs—any one particular area, neutralize and/or use repellent on that area again.

Black-Fluorescent Light Test

If you are frustrated in trying to find the sources of odors, you might want to invest in a black-fluorescent light that will highlight urine spots invisible to the naked eye. Black-fluorescent lights are available through pet supply mail-order houses for approximately $25 each.

Hang In There—It's Temporary!

If any of this seems overwhelming, remember, if you clean correctly (in conjunction with the rest of the Three-Step Program), the need to clean at all is short term, while the pleasures of owning a housebroken dog continue for many years.

6

Step Three, Part One—
Training: The Paper Chase

Paper Training Young Pups Is Essential for Most Families

Paper training means training your pup to relieve himself on newspapers spread on the floor for this purpose. Paper training is the first stage of housebreaking. Housebreaking means breaking your dog's habit of eliminating in the house, even on paper. The *process* of housebreaking includes a temporary continuing use of paper.

Taking your pup outside before he is three months old is dangerous because he is too susceptible to disease. Nor is he able, at this young age, to hold his urine and stools when left alone for many hours; he will need to relieve himself frequently, especially after eating, drinking, playing, and sleeping.

However, if he's had all his shots before you get him—or as soon as he's had them after he's yours—immediately head for the great outdoors, unless your vet tells you that in your particular situation you should wait a bit longer.

Even with far smaller, considerably more manageable pets, as you will see later, training a pooch to go from paper to the outdoors is actually *re*training, which is never as easy as direct initial training. Don't make any of it more difficult than it has to be for you as well as your pup by waiting any longer than absolutely necessary! If the weather is bad, remember dogs have natural fur coats; if this doesn't seem sufficient, dog sweaters and raincoats are always an option.

The Option of Not Paper Training

Not paper training works only if you are in a position to walk your puppy whenever he has to go—all day, every day. Simply cover his entire room (see next section, "A Room of His Own") with newspaper, instead of only a section of the room, so that you are never showing either approval or disapproval when he goes in the house. This avoids the issue of retraining and the confusion some experience after having been told it was okay to go in the house, only to subsequently learn that it's no longer okay.

If this process works for you, your next step is to simply take up the paper, as soon as he's old enough, and start walking him.

However, paper training frees you from needing to provide more walks than your schedule may allow.

A Room of His Own

Before you bring your pup home, decide which room will be used as his living quarters. This room should be the primary family hangout area so he won't be lonely. Often the kitchen is best because usually the floor is comparatively easy to clean. The bathroom is too constricting, and can give him too long a distance to travel from his play space back to his paper.

Darling was a nine-week-old dachshund who belonged to a single woman in her mid-forties, Elizabeth, who wrote passionate paperback romance novels. Elizabeth also had a Siamese tomcat named Dearest. Dearest's box was in the bathroom, which was where she also put Darling's newspapers. The apartment was relatively small, all on one floor. Certainly, her basic concept seemed reasonable enough: she intended to confine both animals' elimination areas to the same room, where messes could be disposed of conveniently and quickly with a minimum of unwelcome odors wafting through the rest of the apartment. From the first day she brought Darling home, Elizabeth conscientiously got down on her hands and knees and "walked" him, steering her cheerful, waddling little friend into the bathroom, so he'd know where his paper was. But Darling, still small enough to be carried in one hand, never once made it to the paper!

This syndrome, otherwise known as out-of-sight, out-of-mind-newspapers, is all too common. Especially at Darling's age, a pup's memory is extremely limited. Even with considerably older dogs, the operative words are instinct and conditioning, not memory. Although any dog (at any age) can be trained to use a paper, first he's got to find it! To expect any pup to remember an out-of-sight location really isn't fair, especially in the new environment of your home which almost always is so much bigger to him than it ever could seem to you.

Limit His Freedom

To clarify your pup's options for him (and to keep yourself from going nuts by trying to keep track of him every minute!), decide which room is to include his initial living quarters, and block it off from the rest of the house with a mesh or accordion gate. (As mentioned earlier, pay attention to the size of the accordion openings so you won't select one in which he may catch his head.) Or you may construct a homemade barricade. Whatever you use, make sure he can see out so he won't feel isolated. Also, it's important that whatever you select be sturdy. Never underestimate the strength of even a small pup who is unhappily blocked off, and determined to get to where the action is!

Sectioning His Area

Divide his living quarters into two sections, one for living and the other for elimination. He must be able at all times to move freely from one to the other, and to see his newspaper.

Living Area

In his living area will be his bed and his food bowls. As mentioned previously, dogs are denning creatures and feel secure when given their own warm, quiet space. His bed should be a box or crate, either homemade or store bought, with some sort of padding on the bottom. Be sure to consider his adult size when purchasing an expensive bed!

Elimination Area

Directly opposite his living area, place newspapers or house-breaking pads (commonly used for small breeds, but also available in extra large sizes), found in pet stores. The pads are more absorbent with no ink mess, and the plastic lining protects floors. Initially, cover an extra large area with paper, filling one-third of his living space. Lay the paper lengthwise and give an adequate amount to allow him to use it twice comfortably. The larger the pup, the longer the paper. Pups have a natural urge to go away from their own dirt, so change the paper often; otherwise, you are encouraging the "just missed the paper" problem.

Place paper in one area only, never in other rooms of the house. This mistake is common among new owners. The pup should have only one elimination area.

If—and *only* if—he consistently soils outside of the paper-covered section, leave a soiled sheet under the fresh paper; thus, his nose will help draw him to where you want him to go.

After several days, decrease the size of the paper-covered area, shrinking down as you aim toward a convenient place or toward an exit door from which eventually he will be let out or taken out for walks.

Limited Play Time Elsewhere

In the beginning, it's okay to bring him into another room for short play periods. Wait until he relieves himself, and then

allow only fifteen to twenty minutes away from his designated elimination area. And be patient! "He only had one
accident last week," a client told me over the phone. "Can't
we start letting him sleep in the kids' rooms?" In a word,
no! At least not unless they were ready for a major backslide
on the progress already made.

Correcting During Paper Training

The key to effective correcting is prevention rather than discipline. If you've followed all the guidelines laid out so far,
going off the paper will become a rare occurrence, indeed.
When—if—it does happen, remember, during these early
weeks your pup is still a baby. Don't frighten him; be gentle! If you catch him during an accident, quickly pick him
up, and say—don't yell—"no," then carry him to his paper and
verbally praise him while he finishes. Do not pet or touch
him in any way while he goes; touch will only distract him.

Later, this soft approach changes dramatically. You will
have to be tough, because as he grows older and is capable
of more sophisticated behavior, much more will be expected
of him.

Caution!

Be careful. It is during the paper training phase of the overall training process that most people set themselves up for
later problems by failing to prevent or at least eliminate all
indoor odors. Nothing is more likely to cause a dog just
beginning the outside phase to regress to earlier indoor transgression patterns on your floor! If you believe you may have
missed any odors, refer back to Chapter 5 to learn how to

detect the presence of and to fully clear away odors. An odor is a powerful canine incentive to repeat soiling in areas he has already "marked" as his.

Paper Training Exclusively

Although I do not believe this is a good idea, it is worth mentioning that sometimes owners of small breeds choose to remain permanently with paper training as an alternative to outside training. This can be very difficult because you are in fact teaching him to soil in the house. Especially males tend not to "get it" on the distinction between the paper and other parts of the house. In these cases, defining the paper area by partitioning it off from the rest of your home or using a crate or cat-litter pan may be necessary.

Correcting the toy breed pet must be done without shouting as they are easily frightened and thus distracted from the lesson. Roll or shake a wrapped "throw can" instead of tossing it, or gently clap your hands for a similar effect.

Difference Between "Paper Training" and "Housebreaking"

The following chapter defines the line between paper training and housebreaking. Although both generally are lumped together under "housebreaking," in fact paper training is the first step in housebreaking. In the paper training stage, teaching your dog to use the paper is an end unto itself; all you are doing is defining an acceptable elimination area for him within your home.

Housebreaking means breaking him of his habit of going in the house, even on paper. It is training him to go outdoors instead. In the early stages of outdoor training, you'll still use the paper sometimes, but only in support of your new goal.

Are You Ready?

Outdoor training is a joint venture. Your dog needs to be ready, willing, and able to hold between walks. You must be available to watch him and to walk him when he needs it. Much of this you can control by what and when you feed him. If no one is home most of the day on most days, plan to initiate the switch over a weekend when you will be able to give it your full attention.

7

Step Three, Part Two—
Indoor Support for
Outdoor Training

Pups React Differently

Each pup will respond differently to outdoor training. Some, with just a good schedule of feedings and walks, will easily adjust, while others will not accept change easily and therefore will need additional techniques, requiring all the patience you can muster. In addition, some will need more walks than others, but even this will change as they grow older and become better able to hold for longer periods of time.

Observation Chart

Before creating the schedule which eventually will serve as the foundation for your housebreaking routine, take a few days to observe your pup's indoor elimination patterns. Knowledge is power; the more predictable he becomes, the easier he will be to train. Tear out and make some photocopies of the "Observation Chart" and "Schedule" in Chapter 10. When you fill out the observation chart, pay particular attention to the time span between eating and elimination. This information will tell you how to best schedule his feeding times and when you should schedule walks.

As your pet grows older, continue to observe when he needs to be walked, and update a "Schedule" copy accordingly. Month by month throughout his first year, his habits will change and he will become able to hold for longer periods. Please note that very young pups—three to four months—also need to be walked after sleep and after play. At this age, they have little control. However, as your chart will indicate, as he grows older, essential outings will be fewer and not as soon after meals.

Effective Scheduling: Your Primary Tool

Your primary tool in switching your pup from paper to outdoor elimination is effective scheduling, knowing and following through on when to feed him and when to walk him. You must be especially diligent about when you feed him. Also, it may be helpful to note that it is considerably more difficult for a pup to hold feces than urine.

Using the sample "Schedule" you photocopied from Chapter 10, coordinate feeding and elimination times with your pet's changing needs and abilities. Remember, you cannot compare your pup to any other, either in his early ability to hold or in how cooperative he is. For whatever reasons, some pets need more walks, some fewer, some sooner after meals, some later. If the sample "Schedule" does not meet your needs, create your own.

And, of course, *your* schedule is a factor. When are you ready, willing, and able to give your pooch the support he needs? Remember, if the demands you make on yourself are too harsh, you're setting yourself up for a great deal of unnecessary anger and frustration. This can seriously undermine the long-term loving relationship with your pup that you need to start working on from the first day you bring him home.

Using Paper While You Are Not Home

In the beginning, when frequent outings are necessary, if neither you nor anyone else is available during the day to accommodate, you will need to continue using paper. Even if you are home, if you live in an apartment building or if limited physical energy due to age or health are factors, you also may need to rely on paper until he is big enough to hold longer. But continue to do the best you can, walking him as much as possible.

Don't Take on More than You Can Handle!

As with feedings, walks must be on a schedule. If all you can manage is one in the morning and another in the evening, don't be discouraged. While you are home, take up his paper. As long as he relieves himself during these walks and holds while you are home, you are practicing good housebreaking techniques.

Indoor Guidelines

When you are home, use this opportunity to keep a close eye on your pup, giving him progressively more indoor freedom as he shows you day by day, week by week, just how much he can handle. Start by picking up his paper, making sure that where it was and the surrounding area have been properly cleaned.

When you are not home and your pup is alone without his newspaper, he will become conditioned to either positive or negative behavior; he will learn to not soil or to soil. If, by now—after utilizing everything you've read so far—he is keeping clean indoors with good outdoor scheduling, you may need no further training techniques.

Timing is key! Knowing at what point he is ready to be given freedom in his room—or even unsupervised run-of-the-house without having paper down—is critically important. Although each pup's progress is individual, all pups develop greater control as they grow older, and they become increasingly willing to use that control when properly, consistently trained to do so. Even a few weeks can make a major difference. Continue to keep a close eye on his patterns.

When to Correct

Correct accidents only while they are happening. Punishing after the fact causes confusion and distrust. All he'll know is that you're angry; he will not understand why. If you find a mess on the floor and feel you must do something about it, you can put him in the opposite corner while you clean and complain in a low-key manner; but frankly this is to make you feel better, and that's all it accomplishes.

Don't go even this far if you come in the door after being out for any extended period of time while your pet has been home alone. He will not associate your anger with the accident on the floor, whether it was done minutes or hours ago. Instead, he will merely conclude that you are to be avoided when you first come in.

Common Misconception

When your dog openly relieves himself in front of you, he is not being hostile. Usually, he has no intention of displeasing you; he merely hasn't yet gotten the message. Ironically, this has its advantages. He's making it very easy for you to catch him in the act which, of course, is critical for your purposes. This is the time to use your "throw can" to interrupt your pet, take him out immediately, and praise him when he finishes eliminating outdoors.

Consistency

The difference between success and failure is largely determined by catching each and every accident and using the same correction each time. Even one accident not caught and corrected while in process will suggest to your dog that this is acceptable behavior—and you will have to begin teaching him all over again that it is wrong. Accidents only take a second! You need to anticipate them, and watch your pet. There should never be a question as to his whereabouts. Always, he should be either

1. in sight
2. outside
3. confined

For additional help on how to keep him in sight, see "Indoor Leashing," later in this chapter.

Properly Correcting Accidents

Properly correcting accidents is imperative, even after you see encouraging results outside. If you've caught your pup in the middle of eliminating indoors, probably he has more to eliminate, which makes this an excellent time to walk him. Occasionally, he will be too upset. If so, wait until he calms down before you try again. How many times you will need to do this before he at last makes the connection will differ with each pup. Some will catch on after only one or two corrections, while others will require considerably more.

Negative Reinforcement

A correction is negative reinforcement to end unacceptable behavior. How harshly it needs to be administered depends on your pup's reaction, his sensitivity. Those with high sensitivity, especially toy breeds, may need only a verbal correction, while giant breeds may need the whole gambit. You have three options:

1. voice
2. physical action
3. "throw cans"

Voice

Make an impression! Far too many training failures result from correcting casually.

The key word is, "No!" Learn to shout it in a deep, commanding tone, fully expressing your disapproval. Don't scream. Screaming not only frightens a dog, it also distracts from the main issue. Use "No!" only while the unacceptable behavior is in process, and always use it. With small breeds, simultaneously clapping your hands makes it even more effective.

Praise, a form of positive reinforcement, is equally important. When he goes outside, freely express your delight, but keep it low-key. "Good dog!" is applicable here as soon as the dog has finished eliminating. How much praise is appropriate needs to be regulated by your pup's ability to receive it, which will depend on whether his temperament is excitable or placid.

Physical Action

Shaking him by the collar simulates corrections by his mother, and thus gets his instincts working on your behalf. Do not hit him, even with a rolled newspaper, and don't ever rub his nose in the mess! Both are far too expensive in that they establish distrust of physical contact with you.

"Throw Cans"

If you cannot get physically close enough to catch him in the act, use a "throw can" (see Chapter 3 on making "throw cans"). When tossed at his feet, a "throw can" will get any dog's attention, and stop his transgressing instantly. Because

toy breeds are more easily frightened than their larger counterparts, shake the can instead of throwing it.

But Where Oh Where Had Their Little Dog Gone?

Mop Mop was a five-month-old shih tzu. This is a small dog
(10–15 pounds when fully grown). Mop Mop lived in a very
large house—so large, in fact, that most of the time the family couldn't find him, although unfortunately all too often it
was far too easy to determine precisely where he *had been.*
One of his favorite dumping grounds was under the dining
room table, with the laundry room a close second, although
not one of the four kids and three adults with whom he lived
was ever able to accurately predict where his next surprise
might turn up.

The family grew increasingly frustrated and confused, but
so did Mop Mop! Because catching a dog during the act is
so important in successful housebreaking, no matter how
hard the family tried to follow up after each transgression
was discovered, the only message Mop Mop was getting was
that his owners frequently, irrationally, and unpredictably
were furious at him; that none of them could be trusted.

Indoor Leashing

Solution? Keep Mop Mop on a leash *indoors.* Keeping a leash
on your pup indoors lets you know where he is every minute,
and therefore will make it much easier to catch him when
he misbehaves. It also gives him a feeling of being under control, which is reassuring to a confused animal eager to please

you, the leader of his pack. Create a state of instant togetherness by tying him to wherever you sit, or you even can tie him to yourself while you talk on the phone or read. You also have the option of wrapping the leash around any table leg or other stationary object strong enough to hold him. Or let him run free with the leash on.

With any of these alternatives, probably tighter confinement will not be necessary as often. If he chews the leash, use a rope instead.

For small breeds, a harness instead of a collar will prevent him from hurting himself if the leash gets caught on furniture. If this turns out to be a problem with a larger dog, simply shorten the leash.

Having this close, constant supervision will allow you to take immediate steps to correct your pet's transgressions. This may mean taking him to his paper or outside, depending on his stage of training. This instant feedback will accelerate your puppy's training progress.

Constructive Cluttering

Tony Marino was a widower in his late thirties with three school-age children and a mother-in-law named Viola who turned out to be a godsend in helping him with the kids and the house while Tony worked long, irregular hours running his electrical contracting business. But even Viola threw up her hands at trying to keep the family room of the rambling old house in order. In fact, the clutter generated by her three grandchildren, supplemented by a dozen transient kids who loved hanging out at the Marinos' after school and on weekends, at times seemed simply an unstoppable act of nature.

Often the ironing board was up and almost always laundry, books, and toys were strewn from one end of the room to the other. Meanwhile, their pup, Cocoa, a frisky, friendly, seven-month-old cockapoo (half poodle, half cocker spaniel)—with short, brown curly hair—thoroughly enjoyed basking in an ocean of adoring attention.

But the kitchen—where Viola regularly made mountains of some of the best cookies I've ever eaten and where Cocoa was still confined overnight and when he was alone in the house—usually was in perfect order.

"It's the one room I have to keep clean," Viola told me, pushing a whole plate of chocolate chip cookies in my direction, which produced immediate amnesia regarding the five pounds I intended to lose. "She is housebroken," Viola continued. "She'll spend hours in the family room with the kids or even in their rooms, with no problems, but she still messes out here! Only here!"

Without even looking, I could imagine the cluttered floors in the kids' rooms!

Throughout all this, Cocoa smiled at me, beguilingly wagging her tail as though I, of all people, might give her a cookie if she played her cards right.

After listening carefully, then double-checking adherence to the feeding and walking schedule, cleaning, and everything else, the solution emerged. Cocoa, it seemed, must have had some Southwestern blood in her, because definitely she loved the wide open spaces!

Solution?

Clutter the kitchen! Bring in furniture, dog toys, empty dog dishes, whatever. Scatter "stuff," especially her stuff, all over the floor, and leave it there. This approach worked for

Cocoa and can be effective in anyone's house. And if the ghost of where your pup's newspaper used to be still seductively haunts him, try putting his bed directly over that spot!

Obstacle Blocking

Obstacle blocking is a more targeted extension of the concept expressed above. If your pup simply will not give up a particular spot despite your use of every other tool mentioned so far, including repellents, place a physical obstacle directly over that spot. It can be a chair, or perhaps his bed. "Throw cans" also work, especially if you've already introduced him to them through his earlier training. A "throw can" will bring a negative association to what he previously experienced as pleasurable. If the spot is large, string several cans together to encircle it. With this setup, any approach will create a great deal of negative reinforcement noise. However, never use "throw cans" in his living quarters. Here, he must feel secure, not threatened.

Firmer Measures—Strict Confinement

When you restrict your dog's freedom to a severely limited part of his larger overall living quarters you strongly utilize his natural instinct not to sit in his own dirt. You may use a crate, gate, or other form of barricade or tie him on a short leash—all are valid options. When you use a gate or barricade, be prepared, if necessary, to lessen his available space by moving these. Of course, to control his space with a leash, all you need to do is shorten or lengthen it. When using a leash, simply select a convenient area in the room or in a hallway, place an eye hook on the bottom of the wall and attach his leash to it, using one that has a snap at both ends. Technically these are known (in case you're asking for it from a pet supply vendor) as tie-out leads. In this case, this would be an *indoor* tie-out system.

His size is a major consideration; a large dog will need a crate or to be leashed, since gates and other comparable barricades probably will not be sufficient to restrain him. For a small or toy breed, use a harness.

Again, confining your pet so he will have to soil his living quarters will reinforce his desire to hold until he can properly eliminate.

Dealing with Resistance to All Forms of Confinement

So that you will be available to deal with his innate resistance to all forms of confinement, begin practicing when you are home. Limit his freedom for fifteen-minute intervals at first, gradually increasing the time. Reward positive behavior with praise and a favorite toy or rawhide bone and, as long as he doesn't dirty it, make him comfortable with a bed.

When necessary to leave him alone and confined for a long period of time, before you go, give him some exercise, then turn on the radio for the company of a human voice in your absence. Also, avoid dramatic exits. A quick good-bye, with a smile, is best.

Getting your puppy used to confinement, coupled with his natural aversion to sitting in his own mess, will make housebreaking faster and smoother.

Increasing Freedom

When using a leash indoors, begin with allowing approximately three feet of play, incrementally lengthening it week by week up to ten feet if he behaves himself. If he does not, then shorten it and begin all over again. Once he has kept clean on the ten foot lead for two weeks, allow him unleashed freedom of the entire room. The same applies to a gate or barricade; increase or decrease his available space as circumstances merit.

When to Use Confinement

Initially, confinement is used to condition him to hold at all, and then to strengthen the length of time he can hold. In this respect also, all pups are different, with some gaining control sooner than others. Your "Observation Chart" will serve as an especially valuable tool in guiding you on when and how long to utilize confinement. No dog should be confined for more than four hours at one time, except at night. Instead, confinement is intended primarily as a tool to help you when you simply cannot give your pet your full attention.

When to Discontinue Confinement

Never continue any confinement if he dirties it; clean immediately and thoroughly. Otherwise, you are conditioning him to remain in his messes, which defeats the purpose of the confinement. Reintroduce confinement as a training tool later when his ability to hold will be stronger or hours left alone will be shorter.

Overnight

Actually, overnight is the easiest time for your pup to keep clean because he is resting and his stomach is empty. When he's shown that he can and is willing to behave appropriately, unless you object he should be brought into your bedroom. This gets him out of his familiar elimination area. In addition, he will feel reasonably intimidated by your presence. Especially if he has not slept all day, probably he will be content to be with you, and should sleep soundly all night. Bring his bed with him, as a touchstone of his familiar secure surroundings. If your room is not picked up you may still need to keep him on a leash so he won't gnaw through the night on your favorite shoes!

See the section on "Fine Tuning to Accommodate Your Pup's Age" and the section on "Overnight Control" in Chapter 10.

Telling You He's Gotta Go

Not all dogs instinctively bark at the door to alert you to when they need to go out. Some merely pace, while others— dead giveaway!—start walking in a circle, sniffing the ground.

Learn your pup's particular signals, and always be sure that he is not being punished unjustly. It's not fair to reprimand him if you failed to heed his pleas, or possibly were careless in following any aspect of his schedule.

Supervision Remains Critical

Even as your pup's success rate improves, the key in these early stages remains supervision; he is not yet ready for free run of the house. Finish training in the first room before allowing access to parts of the house with which he is not familiar, and then do so only when you can watch him. Any time you simply are too busy, limit his freedom. Even if you fear his whimpering will break your heart, in the long run this will be much easier on both of you!

8

Step Three, Part Three— Training: The Great Outdoors

Introducing the Great Outdoors

Introduce your pup to the great outdoors either by walking him or providing yard outings for short intervals throughout the day whenever you suspect it may be necessary. The earlier he experiences putting his scent outside, the easier the transition from his indoor newspaper will be. If you are using your yard, you can begin when your pup has had at least two sets of shots, but he's safer if he's had three. If you will be training him to the street, because of the added danger of disease it's important to wait until all of his shots are finished, which generally takes approximately three months. Discuss your individual situation with your vet. Whatever your preferred time frame, do not proceed until you hear that it's okay.

Here, once again, patience is critical. In virtually all cases, by the time you take him outside, he will have been paper trained, which means you are retraining him. Many pups are extremely reluctant to make the switch. Baby was a Great Pyrenees. In case you're unfamiliar with the breed, they are in the same ballpark as St. Bernards in size, usually exceeding 100 pounds when full-grown. For Baby, her first encounter with the backyard evoked love at first sniff. However, even though at age three-and-a-half-months she already weighed more than fifty pounds, one day she still managed to lumber up onto a pile of newspapers stacked at least two feet high and do her "paper thing." To this day, we still haven't figured out how she managed it!

Morning Outing

Whatever your situation, the morning outing is critical, and must be a regular part of your pup's schedule. Mornings are the only time when you can absolutely rely on it that if he held both his urine and feces overnight, he's gotta go. If he initially resists switching to the outside in the morning, nature is on your side.

Of course, you may have wound up with a die-hard who'll wake up and outdistance you by eliminating indoors before you can get him out, but you're still far from defeated. If this happens, confine him the night before, and make a point of waking earlier than he does. Very quietly sneak up on him, then take him into your arms and out the door—fast.

Backyards and Streets

Backyards and streets are the same in that you are using one or the other to get your pooch out of the house. However, when you actually begin outdoor training, the differences become apparent, which is why each has been given its own section in this chapter.

Backyard

Backyard Preparation

There are a number of advantages to a backyard. One is, your pup will be less likely to pick up diseases. Also, simply letting him out is much easier than having to walk him.

However, even if you plan to let him relieve himself in your own yard, be sure he is at least two months old and has had at least two sets of shots, although, as stated before, yet worth repeating, the final say on when your particular pet is ready should come from your vet. When he is ready, clean the designated outdoor area with bleach or iodized salt and hose it down thoroughly before letting him out. Also, sweep up sharp rocks and anything else on which he might hurt himself.

Backyard Training

Probably training your puppy to eliminate in your backyard can be accomplished in only one weekend! Enjoy the convenience of just opening your door, but pups are easily distracted outside, so make sure he's tending to business.

Hours left out in the yard will help him to understand the difference between what's done outside as opposed to inside. The thickness of his coat is a consideration in gauging how well he'll tolerate cold weather. On this issue, nature works with both of you. If he continually is exposed to the elements, he will develop a heavier coat in winter, shedding some of it in summer. Although some pups object—loudly!— to being alone outside, these feelings usually diminish if you don't allow him to throw you off balance. If barking is excessive, command "No! Quiet!" and, if necessary, use a "throw can." If your yard does not have a fence, don't be discouraged. See the section on "Outdoors" in Chapter 3 for tools to help you deal with this situation.

Using Newspaper Outside

When transferring from paper training to yard, bring out a few sheets of newspaper—one soiled—and secure them with rocks. This allows you to choose the area in which your pup will begin and sometimes continue to eliminate. You may walk him in the yard to train him to eliminate in a certain area. The latter program makes cleanup easier and the yard safer for the human members of the family.

Weather permitting, you can leave him out all day (9:00 A.M. to 9:00 P.M.), where you also will feed and water him, according to schedule. Do this for two days. After two days of eliminating outside, your foundation is established. Thereafter, you can remove the paper and begin implementing his elimination schedule by when you let him out. If weather does not permit, then follow the same scheduling techniques described for street training as follows.

Street Training

Avoiding Diseases on the Street

If you walk your pup in the street, your options for protecting him from picking up a disease are more limited, but you can (and should!) regulate excessive stool sniffing.

Transferring Training to the Street

If you are an apartment dweller, transferring is not as simple if your pup has not eliminated outside when very young. Many apartment dwellers wait outside for hours in vain with a pup determined to return to the security of his indoor newspaper. Remaining outside unendingly is not the answer. In fact, fifteen minutes is more than reasonable.

If, after this time span, he still has not produced the desired result, take him back inside, but be prepared to walk him again soon. Pups learn by repetition; always return to the same spot. If he's still simply not getting it, bring a soiled sheet of newspaper with you, placing it wherever you'd like him to go.

Additional considerations come into play, here. Princess was a four-and-a-half-month-old, high-strung, nervous rottweiler. Her owners, two single career women in their late twenties who shared an apartment, made one major mistake. To the front of their building was a noisy, busy street, and this was where they usually took Princess because it also enabled them to stop in stores to pick up whatever odds and ends they needed. Princess not only resisted every inch of the way, she often thoroughly embarrassed them by cringing, flattening her ears, tail between her legs, suggesting to all their neighbors and every passing stranger that these two perfectly respectable-looking women were actually psychotic sadists who beat her unmercifully every time they had her alone. Yet in reality, her owners adored her; in fact, more often than not when they erred in their treatment of her, it was on the side of overindulgence!

As in the case of Tiggy, the black miniature poodle introduced in Chapter 1, Princess's supersensitive hearing—a characteristic shared by all healthy dogs—was resulting in behavioral difficulties. The street noise was just too much and was interfering with her housebreaking training. And in Princess's case, the difficulties were further magnified because even a relatively placid pup—which Princess was not!—can become easily distracted by even moderate commotion. When Princess's route was switched to the far quieter, more peaceful street behind the building, her demeanor perked up and her training pace quickened.

War of Wills—You Win!

Even in an adverse environment, eventually any pup will have an "accident" outside. Praise him, calmly but profusely, each time he goes. Usually, the foundation for the switch from indoors to out is laid by the time he has put his scent outside three times.

How to Walk

As important as when to walk, is how! Remember, much of his training consists of conditioning. You are teaching him to associate a particular set of circumstances with eliminating outdoors. By increasing the quantity of "triggers," you strengthen your reinforcement. Therefore, each time you take your pup out, reinforce his previous training by using the following touchstones to remind him of what is expected of him:

1. Choose one place, a spot that's always clear (near a fire hydrant is a good idea) and quiet, for the nervous pup.
2. Walk in one direction to his elimination place. If you are walking him merely for exercise, go in the opposite direction.
3. Make sure he eliminates completely. If he's distracted and does not finish, bring him back within another fifteen to thirty minutes.
4. Walk him at the same time, every day, regardless of weather. For toy and short-haired breeds, if the weather is not good, get a doggie coat.
5. If he starts to piddle inside the house, pick him up immediately (to stop the piddling) and carry him to his elimination place, pronto.

Eliminate on Command

Some trainers will encourage you to teach your dog to eliminate on command—to establish a trigger word or words that he will associate with eliminating, and thus speed up the process. If this appeals to you, simply use the same word patterns, for example, "hurry up," each time he begins, mingling it with lots of praise as his progress continues.

Trigger words may be useful if you travel a lot and your pup is expected to eliminate in strange places. However, it requires infinite repetition and is not necessary. Most pups eventually do quite well without it.

Hanging in There Through the Ins and Outs!

Immediately in the morning, and thereafter according to his schedule, take your pet outside. If nothing happens after a maximum of fifteen minutes, bring him home and watch him carefully, whisking him outside again as soon as he gives any indication of weakening. He will have to let go!

After he's gone outside for three consecutive mornings, you're on a roll; he will freely eliminate outside at other times, as well.

The Best News

The best news is, except for the need to maintain his schedule—which will become increasingly easier for you as he grows older and needs fewer outings—the rest of his housebreaking training, as mentioned before but worth repeating, is temporary. Interestingly, when older dogs suddenly regress to their prehousebroken days, in virtually all cases, the truth is that they were never completely, properly housebroken to begin with. If you do it right the first time, you'll have a pet you can trust for a lifetime! For retraining an "accident-prone" older dog, see Chapter 9, "Solutions for Special Problems."

9

Solutions for Special Problems

Sometimes special problems are generic to the breed, and sometimes they arise strictly from your particular dog's personality. Whatever your situation, if you're having difficulties not discussed thus far, you'll probably find them addressed in this chapter.

Determining the Cause of the Problem

Ascertaining that your problem is indeed a housebreaking issue and not submissive piddling or territorial leg lifting is important. Also small and frequent urination may indicate physical illness, as does diarrhea, which neither young pups nor mature dogs can control. If either is an issue, an immediate veterinary checkup is in order.

Messing on Your Furniture

Some pups see no significant difference between the surface of a bed or a floor. If your pup has soiled on furniture, chances are that it will happen again. Do not give him the opportunity; keep him off all furniture until he is trained. Simply placing "throw cans" where he's likely to jump can help, as can using a gate, a crate, or an indoor leash.

Leg Lifting

Leg lifting, which you may see as just another way of urinating is, in fact, a dog's way of "marking" his territory—yet another leftover wolf trait.

A number of years ago I needed to go out of town overnight, so I left my male rottweiler with a woman in a wheelchair in a nearby neighborhood whose yard was enclosed with a five-foot-high fence. Although it's always nice to know you're missed, Bruno overdid it by jumping the fence shortly after I'd driven away. His startled keeper, unable to go after him herself, quickly got on the phone, mobilizing her friends to track him down. Finally they located him a couple of miles from the house near an ocean inlet, chased him to the end of a pier, and watched in astonishment as he promptly jumped into the water. Even I had not known he could swim!

Frantically, they commandeered a nearby boat and got him on board, but not for long. After beating them to the shore, he quickly disappeared into nearby woods where they searched for him until after dark.

Unaware of any of this, I cheerfully returned the next morning to find him waiting for me exactly where I had left him, inside the fenced-in area of the woman's backyard. What I did not understand until I'd heard the whole story, was why everyone except me seemed astonished and relieved to discover him there.

How did he do it? How did he find his way back in this neighborhood where he had never been before?

He did it by marking his trail, from the moment he first jumped the fence; by lifting his leg on tree after tree, rock after rock, all the way to the water and, afterwards, through the woods.

The point is, leg lifting has a primeval, critically important purpose. However, if you happen to own a male dog who insists on marking his trail from your kitchen to your living room, understanding "why" is considerably less important than learning what you can do to stop it!

Common Problems with Dominant Male Dogs

A dominant male dog will instinctively mark his territory by lifting his leg. Also, he will mount anything he can get his legs around. If any of this describes your pet, pay extra attention when cleaning. Include the walls and furniture, always finish with a repellent, and hang "throw cans" on the legs of your furniture.

Diligent supervision is especially imperative! As part of your housebreaking regimen, you also may need some formal obedience training with special emphasis on teaching the "Down!" command, to establish yourself as the dominant figure, the leader of the pack.

It can also help to limit his walks to no more than four a day, during which you will need to curtail excessive leg lifting. Use a short leash to take him where you want him to urinate, stay until he does, and tug him off-balance when he tries to lift his leg at other locations.

Neutering—which in most cases is a good idea anyway—can do much to suppress this innate, instinctive inclination.

Piddling

"Piddling" is urinating when excited. Normally, this is common among high-strung, sensitive female dogs. In contrast with the dominant male, piddling is a female's instinctive indication of submission, usually occurring when she welcomes you—the leader of her pack!—home, or when you reprimand her.

For the young pup this problem usually disappears in a relatively short period of time.

Solutions for Piddling

Piddling beyond young puppyhood can be the result of either an innate tendency, or of long-term improper correcting, which created confusion and distrust in your actions. Here, once again, formal obedience lessons may be necessary. In this case, place particular emphasis on positive reinforcement, which will help her to build self-confidence and restore trust in you.

In addition, when you greet her at the door, keep it low-key, with no touching. Instead, immediately give her a favorite toy, to divert her attention.

Unfortunately, this is an area in which individual dogs can be vastly different, which makes it impossible to forecast even a remotely accurate time frame on when the problem will be solved. But it will disappear eventually, although in some cases, you will always need to calm her and avoid immediate physical contact upon arriving home.

When He Just Won't Go Outside— Using Suppositories

If he just won't go when you've got him outside, try using baby glycerine suppositories, or two or three matches (cardboard—not wooden) which have never been lit. Dogs respond to the sulphur. Straddle him, bracing him with your legs, while you insert either the suppository or the head-first matches. Usually, if his body is ready to let go of accumulated feces, this works immediately; if not, give it a brief rest, then try again. This is a short-term tool. Once he gets the idea, it will no longer be either necessary or advisable.

Regression When Bringing in a Second Dog

The Stein family—Aaron, Rebecca and their three children— loved Biscuit so much that they decided to get another pooch. They wanted to double their fun and also to cut back on the fighting among the kids as to whose room the dog was to sleep in on any given night. Another goal was to eventually allow the new dog—a female named CC (short for Cupcake)—to have pups. The dogs were both purebred shelties. The problem was, from the day CC arrived, Biscuit regressed.

"I guess it's emotional," Aaron, a professional psychologist, told me. "Jealousy, and all that . . ."

"Not quite," I thought, although my verbal response was considerably more tactful. The real problem was that Biscuit picked up CC's scent every time CC had an accident and, responding instinctively to this call of the wild, he simply got carried away. Solution? CC's housetraining needed to be carried out in tandem with Biscuit's retraining. Biscuit needed the same diet and the same schedule as CC. With this resolved, both dogs soon were doing just fine!

Regression Under Other Circumstances

Even with only one dog, regression can occur quite commonly during the initial housebreaking training, and often for no apparent reason. Don't be discouraged! If the dog is healthy, continue with your regular techniques, and soon the sudden surge of accidents will be only a memory.

Sometimes regression can be triggered by one simple legitimate accident, renewing an old habit. Immediately, reestablish strict schedules and increase your supervision.

Regression also can be triggered by major changes in your pet's routine, such as a stay in a kennel, moving to a new home, or adjusting to a new pet in the house. Anticipate this, and counteract by controlling water intake along with more walks a short time afterwards, and extra attention.

Paper Ripping

This annoying habit is typical of pups that have been confined in pens with shredded paper, as in most pet shops, for long periods of time. The shredded paper has become his toy, while you, of course, need him to take it seriously, leaving it in one piece.

Solution? Provide him with other toys, but know in advance that this alone may not be sufficient. Therefore, in addition to his usual playthings, tie a rag or a Buddha toy—a long twisted rope—to a stationary object in some easily accessible location. The kind of tugging this sort of toy engenders simulates the same action employed to rip paper. Introduce it to him as a game; you tug on one end, let him work on the other. After you're sure he's gotten the idea, take it away, returning it only when you go out or to sleep.

It can also help to tape down the edges of the housebreaking paper.

Unhousebroken Older Dogs— the Problem

The primary hurdle in housebreaking adult dogs, a year or more in age, is that you must overcome a long negative habit. Even though there may have been substantial periods, even months, when he was accident free, reality is that he was never completely housebroken to begin with. In most cases, he enjoyed the luxury of continuous accidents without being caught, and therefore has no good reason—to his way of thinking—not to continue in this same pattern.

If your adult dog—one year or older—has had even one accident a month for the last two months, officially he is not housebroken, and you must deal with this immediately!

With adult dogs, controlling elimination is not the issue; the habit is.

Unhousebroken Older Dogs— the Solution

When training an adult, you are actually retraining. In effect, you must go back to the beginning, following the same rules needed to train a young pup, except that with an older dog you don't have to wonder how long he can hold. He can hold all day or all night; certainly he is ready and able. Your goal is to make him willing!

Adults are also easier than puppies because it is not necessary to run them outside after each correction. Three to four outings per day are ample.

In any week your dog has a second accident, immediately implement nighttime confinement for two solid weeks: no exceptions, no early release. This will initiate a replacement behavior pattern—the habit of not soiling. For no less than two months, during the day, when he is not confined, follow up with strict supervision to catch him in the act and immediately institute proper correction lest he quickly fall back into what quite appropriately might be called an attitude problem. With an older animal, the war of wills can be considerably stronger. He's accustomed to going when and where he wants, in contrast to puppies that, in the beginning, of course, have no established patterns. Often an older culprit will deliberately sneak off to commit his crimes, which may necessitate some spying to catch him. The results are well worth the extra effort.

Be patient! By far, in most cases failure to train an adult dog rests in his owner's willingness to be lulled into a false sense of security much too soon.

Special Considerations with Toy Breeds

At adulthood, most toy breeds weigh under fifteen pounds, and are the most common to retain housebreaking problems even when full grown. Most owners contribute to this by delaying training their delicate pup because of concern over cold weather and outside diseases. To rectify this, you will need patience, retracing all of the steps already outlined in this book. Toy breeds are especially difficult because they are so small and therefore, it's easy to lose track of them. Always, while training, keep them with you, by leashing, by using a pet carrier, or through other restraints.

Last-Ditch Tip—Change the Environment

In those extremely rare cases where a pup reaches six months and still is being difficult, changing his living quarters can be effective. His soiling habit will have become associated with a particular place. In conjunction with confining for two weeks, an older pup can be given virtually a brand new start on his housebreaking regimes.

10

Ready Reference Information

What This Chapter Contains

This chapter offers a review of all major points covered in the book, and also specific details, including sample charts and schedules, on numerous points raised but not expanded upon in the preceding text. At the end of the chapter are two forms: an "Observation Chart" and a "Schedule." I suggest you tear them out of the book and photocopy them, taping them to your refrigerator to be replaced—updated weekly—as your pup grows and changes.

Ground Rules for Outings

In the following, yard outings are lumped together with street outings, under the heading of "walks." Feel free to rearrange whatever you find here according to whatever is

necessary to fit your individual pup's needs and your particular lifestyle. For example, if you must be at a workplace dis-
tant from where you live and no one else is home, you cannot
provide the ideal quantity of water and walks. However, on
weekends and holidays when you are in a position to give
him considerably more direct supervision, do so! Especially
in the beginning, this is critical.

Of course, if you live with others, the burden will be
lighter if responsibilities can be shared. Be clear on who is
committed to doing what and when. Confusion after the fact
as to who was supposed to have fed or walked him is grossly
unfair to your pup.

Sample Basic Requirements for Six-Month-Old Pup

    1. Food, two times a day

    2. Water, four times

    3. Walks, five or six times

Suggested Schedule

6 30	7:00 A.M.	First walk (don't make him wait!)
7 00	7:30 A.M.	Food and water
8 00	8:30 A.M.	Walk
11 30	12:00 P.M.	Water
12 30	1:00 P.M.	Walk
	3:00 P.M.	Walk (optional)

5:00 P.M.	Food and water
6:00 P.M.	Walk
8:00 P.M.	Water (small)
10:00 P.M.	Last walk

Fine Tuning to Accommodate Your Pup's Age

Three-month-old	Water	10:00 A.M.
	Walk	10:15 A.M.
Five-month-old	Water	10:00 A.M.
	Walk	10:30 A.M.
Eight-month-old	Water	10:00 A.M.
	Walk	11:00 P.M.

Overnight Control

The chart below reflects overnight control in compliance with a strict feeding/walking schedule.

Age	Overnight Control
Three months	0 percent
Four months	50 percent
Five months	70 percent
Six months and older	100 percent

Basic Yard Setup

Dog Run

If you chose not to give him your entire yard, a dog run can be installed reasonably inexpensively. A dog run consists of chain-link fencing, which can be bought in sections from a fence shop. Simply look in your Yellow Pages for "fence." Foldable exercise pens also limit his room to roam, but are not as sturdy nor do they allow as much space as dog runs. These can be purchased through pet shops and pet supply mail-order catalogues.

Food and Water Dishes

As mentioned earlier, to prevent insects from invading his food and water dishes, place his food and water in their respective bowls, then place each bowl inside a larger bowl containing an inch or two of water. Insects will not be able to cross the "moats" to reach your pet's food and water. Or, if you're not a do-it-yourselfer, you can purchase a bowl designed on this principle in certain pet shops.

Mats

If your backyard is concrete, always supply an outdoor mat. Concrete is brutal on dogs, especially in winter, and gives calluses to short-coated breeds. Placing cardboard or a pallet underneath the mat will give additional insulation.

Covering

Provide covering from the elements—rain and snow in winter and the hot sun in summer.

Dog Houses

If you plan for your pet to be outside for long periods, a house is best. They can be purchased at fence or pet shops, or they can be homemade. To do it yourself, the large wooden pallets on which material is stacked at markets and soda outlet stores are helpful, and often the owners will simply give them to you, glad to get rid of them. These are especially good because they not only get your pup off the ground, it also is easy to attach sides and a roof to them. Instead of a front door, I recommend heavy plastic strips which will enable him to move in and out with virtually no effort. Keep it simple! As long as it gives him the option of shelter whenever he wants it, you've succeeded!

Summary of the Three-Step Program

Appropriate Feeding (see Chapter 4 for complete instructions)

1. Use quality foods, to minimize quantity of stool and frequency of need to eliminate.
2. Provide meals that your particular pup finds satisfying to ensure quick and consistent feedings. Remember, if he dawdles, take it away. At his next feeding, be assured he will finish within the allotted fifteen minute time frame.
3. To condition your pup's elimination patterns, make food and water available to him only on a strict schedule. Never use off-schedule food as a reward.

Thorough Cleaning (see Chapter 5 for complete instructions)

1. Avoid any cleaning solution containing ammonia.
2. Use neutralizers, not merely cleaners.
3. For hard-to-deter spots, use repellents.
4. Use blocking techniques to reduce the size of large areas and to discourage your pup from returning to problem spots.

Diligent Training (see Chapters 6 through 8)

1. Observe his elimination habits and, based on the information you collect, create—and follow!—an appropriate schedule.
2. Condition your pet with confining techniques.
3. Know your pup, with special consideration for his age; how long is he able to remain accident-free?
4. Begin training using only one room at a time.
5. When you are allowing increasingly more freedom, supervise!
6. Correct accidents consistently, immediately, and only while happening. Never "rub his nose in it." Never shout. Never hit.
7. When you correct, make an impression! Do not hesitate to utilize the "throw can."
8. Use weekends for all-day yard training.
9. Utilize short and frequent walks rather than lengthy outings.

Shopping List

Regular Store (as Opposed to Specialty Vendor)

1. White vinegar
2. Baking soda
3. Paper towels
4. Sponges
5. Rubber gloves
6. Large water pail
7. Soda cans for "throw cans"
8. Tape (to seal the tops of the soda cans when you turn them into "throw cans")
9. Supplies to create a dog house

Pet Shop

1. Bowls
2. Food (remember to read the labels!)
3. Collar or harness and leash
4. Dog coat
5. Poop scoop
6. Bed
7. Crate
8. Toys
9. Outdoor mat
10. Gate (also available through home supply vendors)
11. Neutralizer and/or repellent spray (indoor training)
12. Tie-out system (both indoor and outdoor training)
13. Yard deodorizer (outdoor training)
14. Finished dog house

Housebreaking Worksheets

Observation Chart
fill in time of day

Food	Water	Defecate	Urinate

Schedule
fill in time of day

Walks	Water	Food
_____	_____	_____
_____	_____	_____
_____	_____	_____
_____	_____	_____
_____	_____	_____
_____	_____	_____
_____	_____	_____
_____	_____	_____
_____	_____	_____
_____	_____	_____
_____	_____	_____
_____	_____	_____
_____	_____	_____
_____	_____	_____
_____	_____	_____

The Rest Is Up to You!

You now have all the information you'll need to successfully housebreak your pup. The rest is up to you. You need the patience, discipline, and love to follow through. *Tough* love, in fact. It's not always easy to maintain solid housebreaking principles when that wide-eyed vulnerable little ball of fur tells you in no uncertain terms that his heart will break if he can't have even one between-meal snack, and he doesn't want to be confined! These are the moments in which it is most important to remember that, if you don't housebreak him, you may have to get rid of him and the odds are overwhelming that no one else will want him! So, be tough! Housebreak him!

And on behalf of your dog, for all the wonderful years to come which both of you will enjoy because he is housebroken—thank you!

Epilogue

The following section, entitled "Common Pitfalls," warns of the most common mistakes made by well-intentioned but improperly educated (or improperly disciplined!) owners.

The second section, entitled "Checkpoint Quiz" is designed as a fast trouble-shooting review.

Common Pitfalls

1. Loosing trust by overcorrecting, or correcting too harshly (pay special attention to your pup's age—babies need gentleness!). Also in this category is correcting after the fact, rather than during the unacceptable behavior.

2. Allowing inappropriate behaviors to become habits (often through laziness!). Usually, three corrections (or lack of same) are enough to make or break a habit.
3. Impatience—trying to give too much freedom too soon. (This includes trying to do too much at one time, only one of which is watching your pup. If you can't give him your full attention, confine him or put him outside!)
4. Overly humanizing your pet. Try staring at him for one full minute, then remind yourself that although you can remember all of that minute, your dog can't.
5. Spoiling him during housebreaking, feeding off schedule, and allowing "exceptions" to the no-people-food rule. Undisciplined owners create undisciplined pets.
6. Failing to educate and discipline children in how to relate to your dog.

Checkpoint Quiz

Answer all questions with a "yes" or "no."

Food and Water

1. Are you using quality food to reduce stool amounts?
2. Have you chosen a satisfying food to encourage quick and consistent feeding habits?
3. Are you training your pet to eat and drink at certain times of the day and allowing a time limit for each meal?

Cleaning

4. Are you neutralizing when cleaning and taking advantage of repellents for problem spots?

Training

5. Have you formed a schedule of feeding and walking that works for both you and your pet?
6. Are you catching and properly correcting all accidents?
7. Are you using and not abusing confinement methods?
8. Are you designating appropriate outdoor areas?
9. Are you allowing sufficient outdoor time during walks?
10. Are you exercising your pet adequately?
11. If necessary, are you implementing an obedience program to prevent recurring problems?
12. Are you exercising patience in reaching your goal of housebreaking your pet, without sacrificing his trust in the two of you having a team relationship?

All answers should be "yes."

Index